6·45

Transport

ISSUES
(formerly Issues for the Nineties)

Volume 15

Editor

Craig Donnellan

Independence

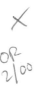

First published by Independence
PO Box 295
Cambridge CB1 3XP
England

British Library Cataloguing in Publication Data
Transport – (Issues Series)
I. Donnellan, Craig II. Series
388

ISBN 1 86168 117 8

Printed in Great Britain
The Burlington Press
Cambridge

Typeset by
Claire Boyd

Cover
The illustration on the front cover is by
Pumpkin House.

CONTENTS

Introduction

Transport is the fifteenth volume in the **Issues** series. The aim of this series is to offer up-to-date information about important issues in our world.

Transport looks at the current transport problems and the search for solutions.

The information comes from a wide variety of sources and includes:
Government reports and statistics
Newspaper reports and features
Magazine articles and surveys
Literature from lobby groups
and charitable organisations.

It is hoped that, as you read about the many aspects of the issues explored in this book, you will critically evaluate the information presented. It is important that you decide whether you are being presented with facts or opinions. Does the writer give a biased or an unbiased report? If an opinion is being expressed, do you agree with the writer?

Transport offers a useful starting-point for those who need convenient access to information about the many issues involved. However, it is only a starting-point. At the back of the book is a list of organisations which you may want to contact for further information.

*****

What's the problem with traffic?

Information from Friends of the Earth

Over the past century the car has become a part of everyday life; in fact, it's hard to imagine life without it. Most of us think about what the motor vehicle has done for us: it has enabled us to do the shopping, to transport goods, see our friends and family, and go on holiday. But as Britain becomes more and more congested, and our major cities are snarled with all-day traffic jams, it's time to think not about what the car has done for us, but what it is doing *to* us.

More and more of our everyday journeys – even the shortest of trips which could easily be walked or cycled – are being made by car. Almost one in three journeys under five miles in our big cities are made by car. Outside of towns that figure increases to one in two. For some people, especially those in rural areas, cars are increasingly becoming the only way to get around. Meanwhile, people without cars are left behind, isolated, or denied access to shops and services, such as hospitals.

Despite the freedom and mobility the car has brought to us, it has also brought daily tragedy. Road accidents are the single biggest killer of children under 15; key wildlife sites are under threat from road building and pollution; and communities are divided by busy roads. The air we breathe has become polluted with health-threatening gases such as nitrogen oxide, ozone and benzene, produced by the burning of car and lorry fuel.

And it's going to get worse. Road traffic is predicted to increase by 38 per cent in the next 15 years. The Department of Transport's National Road Traffic Forecasts predict an increase in road traffic of up to 75 per cent between 1996 and 2031. Much of the time we already spend in cars is actually spent going nowhere. On average UK drivers spend 5.4 days each year just sitting in traffic jams. Congestion is costly, too: it's been estimated that traffic congestion costs UK industry some £15-20 billion every year.

You might think building new roads would ease the congestion, but studies show that building new motorways or widening existing roads often leads to an increase in traffic and therefore to more congestion.

Friends of the Earth recognises that we can't turn back the clock: cars and lorries are here to stay. We can build cleaner, safer vehicles. We can invest in public transport and use it more. But in the long run we can cut pollution and other negative effects of road transport only by cutting traffic.

Every breath you take

In 1998, new air pollution figures released by Friends of the Earth showed that in some areas of Britain Government health standards for levels of air pollution were being broken as often as once a week. This means that the air is not fit to breathe. In most of these areas, the main source of pollution is road traffic.

Road traffic – cars, lorries, motorcycles and coaches – is the fastest-growing source of air pollution in the UK today. Traffic fumes are responsible for the increasingly frequent smogs which pollute not only our towns and cities but also our rural areas.

The air we breathe

In many parts of the world the air people breathe is killing them. According to *The Times of India*, in Bombay and Delhi, for example, breathing the urban air every day is the equivalent of smoking 20 cigarettes, mainly because of traffic.

Think it's not a problem here? Over a third of the UK population lives in areas where European health standards for air quality are regularly

breached. Air pollution is a serious threat to human health, especially to children and the elderly, pregnant women and people already suffering from heart or lung disease. The Government now accepts that up to 24,000 people die prematurely every year as a result of exposure to air pollution.

When pollution levels are high, road transport is usually responsible. Pollutants in our air linked to road traffic include particulates, nitrogen dioxide, carbon monoxide, benzene and ozone. Benzene is a known cancer-causing chemical. Particulates – tiny particles of dust and pollution – are linked with respiratory problems and lung damage.

Asthma

The incidence of asthma in the UK has doubled in the last 15 years. Asthma kills around 2,000 children and adults each year, and the number of children admitted to hospital for asthma more than doubled between 1976 and 1998. We know that air pollution aggravates asthma, and may trigger an attack.

The trouble with cars

The car shapes our whole existence: cars and car use affect where we live, where we shop, how we get to work, and even whether we consider ourselves poor or wealthy.

Inequality

It's accepted wisdom that the car has improved our quality of life. But the car has also contributed to the widening gap between the rich and the poor in Britain, and it remains a symbol of inequality world-wide.

Eighty per cent of the world's cars are owned by less than 20 per cent of its people, mainly those in richer nations. There are more cars in just one US city – Greater Los Angeles – than in the whole of India, China, Indonesia, Pakistan and Bangladesh put together.

In the UK roughly a third of households do not have access to a car. In the last twenty years car mileage for shopping has tripled, largely thanks to the rise of the out-of-town superstores. Dozens of these supermarket/DIY/multiplex shopping parks are built every year.

If people without cars want to shop at supercentres they have to put up with poor public transport provision. Transport to shopping malls is poor because the people who build them count on customers arriving by car – a recent survey at Asda near High Wycombe, Bucks, found that of 236 customers interviewed, only four did not come by car. People without access to a car have to shop in the increasingly deserted inner town areas, where small shop owners have already been driven out by the big supermarkets. Here food is more expensive and there is less choice than in the superstores.

Greenfield housing

Government forecasts say that 4.4 million new households may form in England by 2016. The question of how and where these people will be housed will be one of the most important environmental and social issues of the coming decade.

More and more houses in the UK are being built on 'greenfield' or out-of-town land, a precious resource in Britain, when much derelict and underused urban land could be converted for our homes and flats. Greenfield housing, often far from city centres, leads to increased dependence on the car and to the erosion of Britain's traditional High Street shopping and street market culture.

We have to stop the endless urban sprawl and build homes in towns, where people can use public transport. This will lead to stronger communities, and to a reduction in traffic.

From road rage . . .

'Road rage' is when motorists get so upset by the behaviour of other drivers they literally go crazy, doing injury or even causing death to other drivers. According to a 1996 survey the majority of drivers have been the victim of road rage at some time. This includes over one in six people being forced to pull over or off the road by other drivers and nearly one in ten having had people get out of their car and physically threaten them.

Congestion is forecast to double between 1996 and 2017. You don't have to be an expert to figure out that unless we do something to curb traffic, road rage is going to become more and more a part of a driver's life.

. . . to death

Being killed in a road accident is the most common cause of death for children under 15. Roughly one child in 15 is injured in a road accident before his or her sixteenth birthday.

It's not hard to understand then why fear of accidents has led to a decline in children's freedom. Many parents are now taking their children to school in cars. Fear of traffic accidents has resulted in a virtual imprisonment at home for many young people.

At the same time, play space has shrunk, and parks are often divided from houses by busy roads, which children are not allowed to cross without an adult escort.

Countryside and wildlife pay the price

While cars are choking our towns, much of the UK's remaining road-building is destroying our countryside. In the last 30 years, some of our most valuable wildlife sites have been wrecked by road-building.

In 1993, nationally important wetland meadows and chalk grasslands were ravaged when the M3 was built through Twyford Down. The Department of Transport got even worse press in 1996 when it bulldozed through the beautiful heathland of Snelsmore Common to build the Newbury bypass. Many scarce wildlife species such as dormice, nightjars and rare bats were left homeless or dead, as construction got under way.

But many plans for new road-building have been fought off. The ancient trees of Oxleas Wood in South London were preserved for future generations when residents, helped by Friends of the Earth, forced the Government to abandon a new expressway. In the last five years, over 250 road projects have been cancelled.

Yet the threat of road-building remains. In Bingley, Yorkshire, a new dual carriageway is to be built through Bingley South Bog, home to many orchids and scarce flowers. Plans to upgrade the south coast road near Hastings threaten marshland at Combe Haven and Pevensey. Altogether, the Government wants to build 37 new roads in the next seven years.

Even though road-building has been scaled down, threats to our wild places from the polluting effects of traffic remain. Oil and heavy metals run off major roads into roadside verges, poisoning the area for wildlife. And as animals breathe the same air we do, they suffer the same effects of pollution.

Worse, they get mown down. Every year on our roads one million animals, mainly rabbits, foxes and hedgehogs – and millions of birds – are killed. Badgers are hard hit too, with almost 50,000 killed every year.

Disaster at sea
The destruction isn't confined to our countryside; our coastal waters are being polluted as well. Forty-five per cent of all oil imported by tanker into Britain is destined for use by cars and lorries. In February 1996 the oil tanker *Sea Empress* ran aground off the coast of Wales, spilling over 70,000 tonnes of crude oil. The clean-up cost is estimated to be at least £60 million. Fishing bans were imposed in the area for 18 months following the disaster and sea birds and other wildlife were devastated.

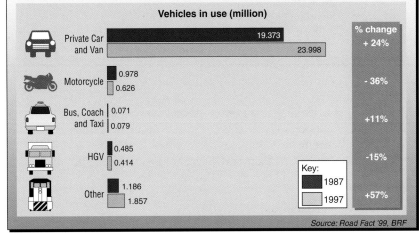

Vehicles and drivers

There are 30 million vehicle licence holders in the UK: 68% of people over the age of 17 hold a driving licence and more than half a million more pass their driving test every year. The graph below shows the fluctuation of the numbers of vehicles in use in 1987 and 1997.

Vehicles in use (million)

Vehicle	1987	1997	% change
Private Car and Van	19.373	23.998	+ 24%
Motorcycle	0.978	0.626	- 36%
Bus, Coach and Taxi	0.071	0.079	+11%
HGV	0.485	0.414	-15%
Other	1.186	1.857	+57%

Key: 1987 / 1997

Source: Road Fact '99, BRF

Stop those roads!
Fortunately the last few years have seen a remarkable turnaround in transport policy. Successive Governments have scrapped hundreds of roads. Yet little has been done to promote alternatives to the car. If millions of homes are built on greenfield sites, a whole new generation of children will grow up dependent on the car. If more road-building is to be avoided, the Government must bring in policies to cut traffic, based on firm traffic reduction targets.

The big picture
What is traffic doing to the planet?
In Karachi, Pakistan, the car population is growing two and a half times faster than the human population and the city has one of the most severe air pollution problems in the world.

In Athens, the famous Parthenon, which is made of white marble and which has survived countless invasions, lootings and bombings, is crumbling due to the effects of air pollution, much of it from Athens' traffic, which gives the city one of the worst congestion problems in Europe.

In Mexico City air pollution from vehicles is so serious that drivers are banned from taking out their cars on one day each week in a system called 'hoy no circula' (don't drive day), each car being identified by a number at the end of its number plate.

Climate change
Global warming is here. Over the last 100 years, average global temperatures have increased by around half a degree. And the evidence is that this rise is accelerating. If we fail to take action, global temperatures may increase by up to 3.5 degrees Celsius by the next century. This could mean a rise in sea level of as much as a metre, causing disaster for low-lying parts of the world, including some areas of the UK.

Global warming isn't just about the Earth getting warmer. As the climate changes, extreme weather events – hurricanes, tornadoes, floods, droughts and heatwaves – become more common. 1998 was a year of extreme weather on a frightening scale, with ice storms in Canada, heatwaves in Texas and Greece, hurricanes, in Central America, floods in Britain – hardly anywhere on the globe escaped the effects of severe weather.

What does all this have to do with cars?
Scientists believe the planet is getting warmer because the industrialised world is pumping more 'greenhouse gases' – substances which cause the heat of the Earth to be trapped, rather than to escape out of the atmosphere – than ever before.

If we want to save the delicate balance of climate on our planet we have to change our ways. It's estimated that if we cut global emissions of carbon dioxide by 60 per cent, then by the middle of the next century we will have a climate the Earth can cope with. That means that, on average, the industrialised nations, including the UK, must cut their CO_2 emissions by up to 90 per cent!

With over 200 new cars hitting the UK's streets every hour in 1996, we have our work cut out if we are to meet this target. We have to wake up to the fact that every time we rev up our motor for a quick trip to the superstore, we are contributing to global climate change, and mortgaging the future of our children.

What Friends of the Earth is calling for

We have to make a personal commitment to cut traffic by first using our cars less for personal journeys; Government and industry must make commitments to getting vehicles off the road too. In the long run traffic simply has to be reduced.

Road traffic reduction

Cutting traffic can actually create jobs, and Friends of the Earth has shown how. We need to develop a sustainable transport system in the UK. The time has come to invest in buses, more trains, more undergrounds with better facilities and fares. Green policies to promote public transport, cycling and walking could lead to the creation of 130,000 new jobs in the next ten years. Most of these jobs would come in public transport and industry.

Friends of the Earth has successfully persuaded Parliament to pass two Road Traffic Reduction Acts to make the Government and local councils set targets to cut traffic levels. FOE believes cuts in traffic of about 10 per cent by 2010 (from 1990 levels) are needed, but the Government has refused to set a target and is planning for more traffic growth.

Funds for public transport

Friends of the Earth wants the Government to invest in improving public transport. For example, buses can carry more people than cars for a fraction of the fuel. But there hasn't been the will so far – and it's no wonder, when over the last 20 years, rail fares have risen by 75 per cent and bus fares by 60 per cent while overall motoring costs have fallen by nearly seven per cent. Government has to make public transport more convenient, more frequent, and extend it to rural areas if people are going to use it.

The big clean up

Because cars aren't going to go away, car and lorry manufacturers, along with oil companies, have got to play their part in the big pollution clean up, by making the engines as clean as possible, reducing the sulphur and benzene content of fuel and cutting down on emissions.

Catalytic converters, devices that cut down on a car's dangerous emissions, are part of the answer. But they take a mile or two to kick in, which is why shorter car journeys are extra polluting. We need to curb our car use for short trips.

Meanwhile, Government should tax polluters by introducing a higher tax for those who drive gas guzzlers. We should also increase our tax on petrol to encourage drivers to use less fuel. Part of this tax revenue can be used to fund public transport as well as other, cleaner types of energy, like sun, wave and wind power. Only if we reduce our reliance on fossil fuels will the planet breathe easier.

Here's what you can do . . .

- Cycle! In Britain only about two per cent of journeys are made by bike, compared to the Netherlands, where about 30 per cent of trips to work are made on two wheels. Here, decades of pro-vehicle road building have squeezed out the humble bicycle. Yet cycling provides a good alternative to driving. In congested cities cycling is often faster, too.
- Leave it at home: If you have a car, whenever possible leave it at home – walk, cycle or use public transport instead.
- Value efficiency: If buying a car, choose a small, fuel-efficient one.
- Find out what your company or employer is doing to cut car travel to work: Do they encourage employees to use public transport or bicycles by offering interest-free loans for season tickets or for buying bicycles? Do they promote car-sharing? If not, suggest such a scheme.
- Get on the bus: If you live in a city, the best way to get around is by public transport; use the bus if you can. Buses can move many more people for a fraction of the fuel.
- Keep informed: If you think the air in your area is particularly foul, ring the Government's Air Pollution Information Service on 0800 556677, look at page 106 of Teletext or pp410-419 of Ceefax, or look up the Government's Internet site: www.environment.detr.gov.uk/airq/aqinfo.htm
- Report dirty diesel vehicles to your local Vehicle Inspectorate Enforcement Office (only for heavy goods vehicles, buses and coaches). Contact the Department of Environment, Transport and the Regions' helpline on 0171 890 3333 for the number of your regional office.

© Friends of the Earth

".. WE NEED TO RETHINK OUR RELATIONSHIP..."

Roads and the environment

Information from the British Roads Federation (BRF)

Roads are sometimes seen as harmful to the environment, but sensitively designed road improvements can enhance it. Most roads were built many years ago and so do not conform to the high environmental specifications that are now available, although there are options for improving environmental performance. Today's modern vehicles conform to stringent European emissions standards and modern engines produce substantially reduced amounts of harmful pollution.

Land take

The entire road network of the United Kingdom covers less than 2% of our land area. Only 1% of the increase in road length in Great Britain over the last decade has been motorway or trunk road. 75% of the increase has been in unclassified roads, mainly in residential and industrial developments, with the remaining 24% on local authority classified roads.

Bypasses

Bypasses bring clear environmental and social benefits to towns and villages by removing through traffic, making communities cleaner, quieter and safer places in which to live and work. For the road user, bypasses make journeys less stressful and journey times more predictable.

There are currently around 550 communities in need of a bypass, but many of the proposals have been withdrawn due to lack of available funding and work on others is unlikely to start until well into the next century.

Environmental performance of roads

Today, new roads are built in line with high environmental specifications that reduce their impact on the human and physical landscape. However, the vast majority of people's lives will be affected by the quality of the infrastructure that is already in place and there are a number of measures that can be implemented on the network to improve its environmental performance.

New road-surfacing materials can considerably reduce the amount of noise generated by traffic. Quiet options are now readily available from both the concrete and asphalt paving industries, with the additional safety benefit of a reduction in spray. In addition, environmental noise barriers alongside motorway hard shoulders can reduce the noise for those living close by.

Good landscaping and planting, such as 'green corridors', can visually improve access to urban areas, and help counter the effects of pollution and there are now a range of recycled materials used in the construction and maintenance of roads.

Fuel efficiency

Over the last 20 years the average fuel efficiency of motor vehicles has improved by 25%, with at least another 10% expected over the next decade. Increased fuel efficiency reduces emissions and in the longer term, new technology offers even greater savings.

Pollutant emissions

A clear distinction must be drawn between pollutants which affect the global atmosphere which have been linked to global warming, and pollutants which affect local air quality, which can have impacts on health and cause damage to vegetation.

The Kyoto Protocol, adopted in December 1997, commits the United Kingdom to reducing our output of 'greenhouse' gases, such as carbon dioxide, methane and nitrous oxide, by 12.5% below 1990 levels in the next ten to fifteen years. Carbon dioxide (CO_2) is the only greenhouse gas where road transport is a major source, currently thought to account for 22% of emissions or about 35 million tonnes and despite the growth in traffic levels, growth in CO_2 emissions from transport is slowing. Domestic and industrial sources make up the overwhelming majority of the remainder.

Pollutants with an impact on air quality include oxides of nitrogen (NOx), carbon monoxide (CO), volatile organic compounds (VOCs), lead (Pb), black smoke and particulate matter (principally PM_{10}). Many of these have been linked to health problems and all are covered by the National Air Quality Strategy (NAQS). In recent years, advances in engine and fuel technology have seen a reduction in levels of many of these pollutants from road transport and the targets set by NAQS mean that reductions are likely to continue.

- The above information is an extract from the BRF web site which can be found at www.brf.co.uk/ Alternatively see page 41 for address details.

© BRF 1999

Pollutant emissions

Pollutants with an impact on air quality include oxides of nitrogen (NOx), carbon monoxide (CO), volatile organic compounds (VOCs), lead (Pb), black smoke and particulate matter (principally PM_{10}). Many of these have been linked to health problems and all are covered by the National Air Quality Strategy (NAQS).

Pollutant emissions from road transport: thousand tonnes

	1990	1996
NOx	1,305	989
CO	4,841	3,313
VOCs	1,170	823
Pb	2.2	0.9
Black Smoke	208	198
PM_{10}	67	52

Source: BRF

UK loves to drive but hates to pay the cost

John Prescott admitted to the *Observer* last week that there would be chaos on the roads for a decade. Now a new study reveals we have the worst transport record in Europe

Britain has one of the worst transport records in Europe for everything from investment to congestion along with a reliance on the motor car that borders on obsession, according to new figures released by the Organisation for Economic Co-operation and Development.

The OECD research reveals that Britain spends less on roads, railways, bus and tram networks and canals per head than most of its northern European neighbours, including France, Germany, the Netherlands, Belgium, Switzerland and most of Scandinavia.

Publication of the findings follow Deputy Prime Minister John Prescott's admission in the *Observer* last week that the nation's roads will continue to be choked for at least the next decade. Downing Street moved quickly last week to deny it was losing confidence in Prescott's handling of the transport crisis.

Privatisation has failed to increase total investment. Even though Britain relies more heavily on the private sector for investment than most other European countries, the total public-private spending record of around £10 billion a year still falls far short of most of its neighbours.

The OECD found that Britain spends less than 1 per cent of its gross domestic product on its transport network, less than Germany, France, Finland, Portugal, Spain, Sweden and Switzerland.

The result is a heavy reliance on the car. An investigation by the European Commission found that Britain relies more on roads – passenger and freight – than any other EU country and, according to the Automobile Association, it has the worst levels of congestion.

By Joanna Walters,
Transport Business Editor

The EC research found that 88.3 per cent of all passenger journeys made in the UK were by car – the highest in the EU – and 11 per cent by public transport. The EU average is 82.2 per cent by car and 15 per cent by public transport.

'Britain has comparatively low car ownership per head in Europe but is the heaviest road user. A major reason is the company car culture which encourages people to make maximum use of their vehicles,' an EU source said.

There is little likelihood, however, of weaning private users from their cars while public transport remains unreliable.

How we compare

Per capita spending per year on 'inland transport infrastructure'

UK		£110
Germany		£200
France		£168
Sweden		£208
Switzerland		£420

Source: The Guardian, June 1999

In a hint that there could be further chaos to come for the country's rail network, Alastair Morton, the new chairman of the Strategic Rail Authority, admitted that Railtrack, the privatised rail infrastructure company, lacked sufficient management expertise to handle big infrastructure projects.

Overstretched Railtrack is being asked by the Government to take on the sub-surface lines of London Underground.

Morton, speaking at the Transport Select Committee last week, said: 'I have serious concerns there are not enough project management skills at this time.'

Morton was especially referring to Railtrack's inept handling of major work along the West Coast Mainline under preparation for Virgin Trains. He warned: 'There is going to be major capital spend on the West Coast Mainline. There will be certain closures and disruption to services. This has got be managed and has got to be managed by good project management by Railtrack and the train operating companies. One of my great concerns is there are not enough project management skills in this pot.'

At the same hearing the new hardline rail regulator, Tom Winsor, revealed that Railtrack now admits it will not be able to meet its commitment to set aside sufficient extra track on the new West Coast Mainline for other train operators.

Winsor, handpicked by Prescott to provide a tougher regulatory regime, said he would be examining Railtrack's failure to meet its obligations on his first day in office on 5 July. He also issued a swingeing attack on Railtrack blaming poor infrastructure for more than half the delays by train operating companies.

He said: 'Railtrack talks a good game. Now they have got to play it. It is not a question of waiting patiently for five years for the next periodic review.

'It is not a question of waiting patiently for Railtrack to raise their game at the time they choose and the way they choose. The public has been patient for long enough. I think the time has come for some impatience. I am impatient for improvement.'

He also criticised his predecessor Chris Bolt, pointing out that not a single enforcement notice had been imposed by the regulator against Railtrack. He warned that, in future, the regulator may use its powers to impose fines, or even seek court orders against Railtrack.

Winsor and Morton are known to be frustrated that it has taken Prescott two years to appoint them and a senior industry source said it was now unlikely they could make a substantial difference before the general election.   © *The Guardian June, 1999*

Transport: what are the issues for the countryside?

Over the last 20 years the distance travelled by car has increased by 55% while walking, cycling and bus travel have all declined dramatically (20%, 25% and 38% decrease). As a result, traffic levels have increased significantly and the Government forecast that traffic could increase by a further 36% – 84% by the year 2031. Traffic levels on rural roads are set to rise more quickly than in urban areas and could treble in some areas. These trends create a number of serious problems for the countryside, including:

- the destruction of landscapes and habitats through road/rail construction;
- global and local pollution from motor vehicles;
- the cumulative erosion of the special qualities and tranquillity of the countryside through traffic increases, safety improvements, night lighting and standardisation of road design;
- the development of new, dispersed, patterns of development which devour countryside and lock people into car-dependent lifestyles;
- growing isolation for the 22% of the rural population without access to a car.

Council for the Protection of Rural England (CPRE) priorities

CPRE is one of the leading organisations campaigning for environmentally sound transport policies. CPRE's overall objective is to reduce traffic and the need for new and widened roads by ensuring that new development – such as housing – is located in places which reduce the need to travel altogether and which are accessible by foot, bike and public transport and that travel costs reflect the impact on the environment. This will require:

- a new approach to locating development which focuses on urban areas first. These areas are more likely to provide employment and services in close proximity to where people live. In addition, they are more likely to sustain public transport services;

- more rigorous implementation of Policy Planning Guidance note 13: Transport (PPG13) which advises against out-of-town locations for new development;
- improved opportunities for people to walk and cycle in safety. Almost a third of journeys are still less than a mile in distance and almost three-quarters are of less than 5 miles – many of these journeys could be done by foot or bike;
- improving the quality and quantity of public transport services;
- measures to increase the cost of travel to reflect wider social and environmental costs. This could include increases in fuel tax or greater use of parking charges as a management measure;
- measures to reduce traffic speeds, improve road safety for all users and to redirect heavy lorry traffic on to suitable roads;
- a more critical approach to new road construction which fits in with land use planning objectives and is subject to effective environmental impact assessment and public scrutiny.

CPRE believes a combination of all of these measures will be necessary to reduce car dependency in future and reduce damage to the countryside.

Campaign opportunities

Transport policy is a key priority for CPRE's work nationally, but there are also many opportunities to make a difference locally. You can:

- scrutinise development plans for policies which might encourage extra car travel. Challenge these by backing up your arguments with the policies set out in PPG13;
- monitor planning applications for their transport impacts. Will they simply encourage more traffic?
- check with the regional office of the Highways Agency (see phone book) about any plans for the development of the national road network. Are there any schemes which cause concern? If so, you can write to the Agency letting them know of your concerns. Copy any correspondence to the Government Office in your region;
- study your County Council's Local Transport Plan in the local library. Let them know what you think of their proposals (good and bad) and inform local councillors of your concerns;
- identify tranquil areas in the countryside where traffic levels are low and highlight the need to protect them;
- ask to be consulted when your local authority is next preparing its Local Transport Plan or development plan. These provide excellent opportunities for promoting cycling, walking and public transport and for challenging damaging road schemes;
- join CPRE's Transport Campaign Group (if one exists in your county) to work with others on this important issue.

© Council for the Protection of Rural England (CPRE), 1999

Rural traffic fear survey

A summary

During the spring and summer of 1999, CPRE volunteers undertook and compiled a survey of users of country lanes. A total of 21 groups from around the country took part and the key findings of the survey are included below.

The survey

- 1,022 people were asked for their views on country lanes.
- 95% of people questioned walk, cycle or ride horses in the countryside.
- 91% were also motorists.

Use of country lanes

- 66% of people said they used country lanes 'sometimes'.
- Although the majority of trips were for pleasure, 28% were for commuting or shopping purposes.

Traffic intimidation

- 65% felt threatened by traffic either all or some of the time.
- 3% feel completely safe from traffic on country lanes.
- 91% felt the speed limit on country lanes – currently 60mph – should be reduced.
- 99% of those calling for a lower speed limit supported a limit of 40mph or less for country lanes. The most popular speed limit was 20mph.

- 72% of people believed that walkers, cyclists and horse riders should have priority over motorists on designated country lanes – known as 'quiet lanes'.

Over 380 country lanes were identified by people as having problems of traffic intimidation. These stem from the volume of traffic, speeding traffic on narrow and winding lanes, recent road 'improvements' to improve sight lines which lead to faster moving vehicles, the impact of HGVs, and the physical damage of verges. Find out more by reading our Charter for Country Lanes.

A selection of comments from individuals

'Sometimes I get the feeling that car users think people should not be walking on roads, not even country lanes.'
Respondent from Avon

99% of those calling for a lower speed limit supported a limit of 40mph or less for country lanes

---

'Too many drivers seem to feel that four wheels dominate over two wheels, feet, hooves or anything else.'
Respondent from Cornwall

'It is dangerous to walk to neighbours or to the post box even in daylight.'
Respondent from Essex

'As a horse rider the traffic gets more every year, especially in this area of fast growing housing and industrial development.'
Respondent from Gloucestershire

'The growth in the number and speed of vehicles is completely changing the rural nature of our lanes. Banks and hedgerows are being destroyed.'
Respondent from Surrey

'The grass verges are quite steep in places. Where the lane narrows I have to scramble up the verge sometimes, to get out of the way of the traffic.'
Respondent from Warwickshire

'When riding on narrow country lanes I feel drivers go too fast when they can't see what is ahead. I am always frightened they will run into the back of us.'
Respondent from West Yorkshire

© Council for the Protection of Rural England (CPRE), 1999

England's countryside

Facing traffic trauma or tranquillity?

Rural traffic levels could rise by over 100% during the next 30 years – far outstripping traffic growth in urban areas[1].

'The fate of the countryside as a place largely free from the traffic problems that have dominated towns and cities now hangs in the balance. Either we grasp the opportunity to introduce new transport choices and tame traffic in rural areas, or we face a future of spiralling traffic, sprawl and congestion.'

This is the stark choice presented by CPRE today as it publishes its report, *Traffic Trauma or Tranquillity?* This reveals two scenarios of rural traffic growth: one showing the impacts of successful urban and transport policies in slowing traffic growth, and the second showing the consequences of a failure to deliver such change.[2]

Regional and county-based traffic growth data across the country is attached.

CPRE's Head of Transport, Lilli Matson, explained:

'There can be no room for complacency. Even with successful policies, traffic levels are forecast to increase in all counties. If transport and urban policies fail or are reversed, the situation could be much worse – with a doubling in traffic on rural roads over the next thirty years.

'In counties like Bedfordshire, Nottinghamshire and Dorset, spiralling traffic levels mean that the chances of finding tranquil countryside or quiet country lanes to enjoy will become increasingly rare.[3] *Traffic Trauma or Tranquillity?* makes it clear just how vital the Government's policies are for stopping urban sprawl and delivering a transport "revolution". If these policies fail it will be the countryside that bears the brunt of traffic growth.'

CPRE is calling on national and local government to:

- stop sprawl and regenerate urban areas by taking a strong stand against traffic-generating developments and acting on the recommendations in the recent report by the Urban Task Force;
- civilise rural traffic with lower speed limits of 40 mph on rural roads and 20 mph in villages and by supporting calls for 'quiet lanes' where walkers, cyclists and horse riders have legal priority over motorised traffic;
- set a national target to reduce traffic levels in both urban and rural areas in the forthcoming Urban and Rural White Papers;
- increase transport choice by safeguarding long-term funding for rural buses and trains and by reducing the need to travel by maintaining local shops and services within reach of local residents;
- influence travel decisions through action to increase the costs of travelling by car in comparison with public transport. The revenues from fuel taxes and congestion or parking charges need to be reinvested in improving transport options in both town and country.

Lilli Matson concluded: 'While debates about the Government's transport and urban policies rage on, it is clear that rural areas cannot wait for action to reduce rising traffic levels. Our report is a clear illustration of the need for radical policies to tame traffic in the countryside.'

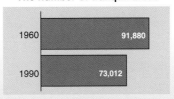

The number of tranquil areas

| 1960 | 91,880 |
| 1990 | 73,012 |

Tranquil areas are places which are sufficiently far away from the visual or noise intrusion of development or traffic to be considered unspoilt by urban influences. They are determined by distances from the various disturbing factors listed below. Deciding on the distances has been an iterative process of comparison between each type of disturbance in the field.

A tranquil areas lies:
- 4km from the largest power stations.
- 3km from the most highly trafficked roads such as the M1/M6; from large towns (e.g. towns the size of Leicester and larger); and from major industrial areas.
- 2km from most other motorways and major trunk roads such as the M4 and A1 and from the edge of smaller towns.
- 1km from medium disturbance roads i.e. roads which are difficult to cross in peak hours (taken to be roughly equivalent to greater than 10,000 vehicles per day) and some main line railways.
- A tranquil area also lies beyond military and civil airfield/airport noise lozenges as defined by published noise data (where available) and beyond very extensive opencast mining.

Source: Council for the Protection of Rural England

References

1. CPRE's research demonstrates that without effective implementation of transport and urban policy proposals, traffic levels on minor rural roads could increase nationally by 104% (1996-2031). In contrast, the Government's *National Road Traffic forecasts* (1997) suggest that urban traffic will grow by 52%.
2. The research for the Traffic Trauma or Tranquillity Map was carried out by Gordon Stokes of Steer, Davies, Gleave on behalf of CPRE. A detailed report on the methodology used in preparing the map is available to the press from CPRE's Press Office on request. The map is available free to members of the public from CPRE Publications, 25 Buckingham Palace Rd, London, SW1W 0PP on receipt of an A4 S.A.E.
3. CPRE recently published its *Rural Traffic Fear Survey* which showed that 65% of people feel intimidated or threatened by existing levels of traffic on country lanes. These problems are likely to intensify as traffic levels rise.

- The above information is an extract from the Council for the Protection of Rural England (CPRE) web site which can be found at www.greenchannel.com/cpre/ Alternatively see their address details on page 41 of this book.
© *Council for the Protection of Rural England (CPRE), 1999*

Britain faces 10 years of traffic chaos

By Joanna Walters and Patrick Wintour

Britain's cities and roads will still be clogged in 10 years' time regardless of radical plans to force people out of their cars and on to public transport, the Government has admitted.

Deputy Prime Minister John Prescott last week conceded to the *Observer* that Labour would need a second term of office before the public could expect 'real and substantial change to the whole transport system'.

Prescott, who is also Secretary of State for Transport and the Environment, is under fire from all sides – including Prime Minister Tony Blair – for failing to overcome the transport crisis.

At a Downing Street meeting last week Blair expressed frustration at the slow progress, including the inability to detail proposals to improve investment in the London Underground. Blair's advisers are worried that Prescott has failed to set transport targets with which the public can identify.

In an ICM poll conducted for the *Observer*, 74 per cent of people questioned said congestion had got worse since Labour took office; 60 per cent said public transport had not improved.

Only 18 per cent thought public transport would improve over the next few years as a result of policies to boost services, while 80 per cent believed there would be as much if not more congestion.

Prescott, one of the most hard-working Ministers, admitted to the *Observer* that he was dissatisfied with the pace of change, blaming lengthy legislative procedures and the long lead times before investment feeds into better public transport.

Asked whether roads would still be choked in 10 years' time, he said: 'There will still be congestion problems. I do not believe we will have a system where you get rid of traffic jams.'

Road traffic is forecast to rise by at least a third in the next 20 years and by half on the motorways – with almost no new roads being built to accommodate it. 'You cannot ban the vehicle in a democracy but I hope a greater priority for public transport will persuade people not to become two-, three- and four-car families,' Prescott said.

74 per cent of people questioned said congestion had got worse since Labour took office

New powers to price people out of their cars and crack down on poorly performing bus and train companies will be central to the legislative programme to be announced in the autumn.

For the first time, all money raised from congestion charging and commuter parking taxes by councils will have to be spent on public transport. But the schemes are not expected to be in operation nation-wide for five years.

Prescott is not to implement a parking levy on out-of-town superstores. Downing Street feared it would alienate business while failing to revitalise declining town centres.

Prescott pointed out he had just unveiled the first motorway bus lane on the M4 near Heathrow Airport. He is soon to announce Britain's first 'Two-Plus' car lane, barred to vehicles with only the driver aboard, on the northern and southern approaches to the Blackwall Tunnel under the River Thames in London.

The Government wants to impose 20 mph speed limits on some country lanes and promote more 'home zones' on urban residential roads, where traffic is discouraged.

A draft Bill to set up the Strategic Railway Authority, aimed at tightening regulation of the privatised industry and boosting investment, is to be published this summer.

© *The Guardian*
June, 1999

City drivers face £7,000-a-year charges

By Paul Marston,
Transport Correspondent

Drivers taking their cars into central London will face tolls and parking surcharges of up to £7,000 a year under proposals put forward by local authority planners yesterday.

Their report, likely to influence councils across the country, concluded that high penalties for motorists represented easily the most effective means of reducing traffic. Improvements to public transport, it said, would have only marginal impact.

It called for the future London mayor to take immediate advantage of the Government's imminent creation of powers to impose charges on road use, and forecast that they could cut traffic by 40 per cent within eight years.

The study, by the joint planning body for all 33 London boroughs, suggested that tolls for entering a central area – slightly larger than the borough of Westminster and the City – should initially be set at £2.50 a day, rising to £7.50 by 2008. A new workplace parking levy would be introduced at £1,500 a year, rocketing to £5,000.

Public car park costs would increase from a typical £10 to £12-£15, reaching £30 by 2008. By then, concentric tolling cordons would cover the whole of Greater London. Drivers moving into the inner zone – between the North Circular and South Circular – would pay £3.75 a day, and those in the outer area – to the M25 – £2.

Toll fees alone are forecast to generate £500 million a year, with parking levies likely to provide at least as much again. The report, published by the statutory London Planning Advisory Committee, said that large cuts in traffic levels were achievable, even with only minor improvements to bus and rail services. Better public transport was a worthwhile goal to redress the 'travel inequalities' between households with and without cars, but it would 'make only a modest contribution to reducing traffic activity'.

The 200-page document found that policy options such as radical fare cuts, more frequent services and new routes would persuade few drivers to give up their cars. A 50 per cent drop in train or bus fares would reduce car usage by only 10 per cent.

Nicky Gavron, the committee's Labour chairman, maintained that the proposals were in line with Government policy and 'not anti-car' as they would speed up journey times for those vehicles remaining on the roads. She said slimming traffic volumes would reduce accidents, noise and 'community severance' while improving air quality and making bus services more reliable.

Launching the report yesterday, Ms Gavron said: 'London can't wait. London really is in a crisis as far as traffic is concerned.' The new mayor had to 'hit the ground running' and would need to work out in advance how to handle the income from congestion charging.

But the proposals were roundly condemned by road-user groups. A spokesman for the RAC said: 'This is all about pricing motorists out of their cars, pure and simple. There is hardly a mention of how the money would be used to improve public transport. Everyone would like to see less traffic on the roads, but you will not achieve it until you give motorists a realistic alternative.'

Richard Diment, director of the British Road Federation, described the study as impractical and superficial. He said: 'The committee has failed to produce a full economic and environmental appraisal to show that its proposals would produce an overall benefit. Simply claiming they would produce "winners all round" without publishing more analysis is unacceptable.'

- Government figures show that traffic levels will rise by more than a third by 2010 even if road charging is introduced, the environment group Friends of the Earth claimed yesterday. It said that Glenda Jackson, the transport minister – who had backed Labour pledges of reducing road use – admitted in a series of Commons questions about carbon dioxide emissions that even if the White Paper for local congestion charging became law, traffic levels would be 37 per cent higher in 2010 than in 1990.

Motor vehicle pollution

Information from the National Society of Clean Air and Environmental Protection (NSCA)

Road transport is an integral feature of modern life, moving people and goods for industry, commerce and pleasure. Over 26 million vehicles are licensed to use UK roads, 21 million of these are private cars. Air pollution, noise, road accidents and traffic congestion are the price we pay for our increasing use of motor vehicles. Traffic causes local pollution problems, filling streets with fumes and noise. Emissions from road vehicles also cause pollution over vast areas of the country, representing one of the largest sources of air pollution, even in rural areas.

Environmental impacts

We must remember that the manufacture and use of millions of road vehicles has other implications for the environment. Both diesel and petrol fuel are derived from oil, a non-renewable resource. At current rates of use, oil supplies could become limited early in the next century. Vehicle manufacturing uses considerable quantities of raw materials such as steel, aluminium, copper, lead, zinc, plastic (derived from oil) and rubber. The extraction and refining of raw materials also has an environmental impact. Building more roads to accommodate the growing burden of traffic consumes energy and aggregates. Once roads have been built, road lighting uses a considerable amount of electricity.

Reducing pollution from road vehicles

There are three approaches to this problem:

- Using engines and fuels which are designed to cause less pollution.
- Limiting use of road vehicles where they are considered to be environmentally unacceptable.
- Planning new buildings and road schemes to minimise pollution.

Reducing emissions

Since 1970 the European Union have agreed a number of Directives progressively tightening vehicle emission limits. These are implemented in the UK through the Vehicle Construction and Use Regulations and Type Approval Regulations. As a result vehicle manufacturers are being forced to improve their design technology to meet the stricter standards.

Catalytic convertors – From 1993 all new cars had to meet limits for HC, NOx, and CO equivalent to those in force in the USA and Japan. This involves fitting a catalytic convertor to the exhaust of the car, which converts the pollutants to less harmful gases. The disadvantage is that catalysts may result in the car using more fuel and increase CO_2 emissions. Catalysts also contain expensive rare metals. Fitting catalysts to existing cars is not always possible and involves major work.

Lean burn – The 'lean burn' engine burns cleaner than existing engines and is more fuel efficient than engines fitted with catalysts. However, so far these have not been able to meet EU emission standards, particularly at high speeds. The challenge for car manufacturers is to develop new engine systems which meet strict emission limits and use less fuel. Evaporation and refuelling emissions can be reduced by the use of carbon canister technology which absorbs HC vapour from the vehicle fuel systems. The EU is currently negotiating legislation which will require this.

Fuels

Unleaded petrol – Leaded petrol will be banned in the EU from 2000. EU legislation ensured that from 1990 all new cars were capable of running on unleaded. This is important as lead interferes with the operation of catalysts and any car fitted with one must use unleaded.

Diesel – EU legislation ensures that all diesel cars meet similar limits for HC, NOx and CO to petrol. Diesels are a source of particulate matter and current limits for particulate emissions are not very strict. It is currently difficult to control emissions from diesels once they are on the road – even if they are producing black smoke. They can

only be stopped if they are causing a danger to other road users by emitting so much smoke that they obscure their vision!

You can report smoky diesel buses and lorries to regional Vehicle Inspectorate Enforcement Offices on the following numbers:

West Midlands 0121 789 7999
Western 0117 9531924
Eastern 0116 276 2411
South Wales 01443 224771
SE & London 0181 665 0885
Scotland 0131 244 6521
North Eastern 0113 288 7818
North West 0161 494 9085

The Inspectorate will then contact the operator, requesting that they clean up their vehicles. Spot roadside checks are also undertaken.

Which is best?

Concerns about health effects of particulate emissions from diesels have given them a less environment-friendly image. Diesel engined vehicles generally use less fuel per mile than a petrol vehicle, but because diesel fuel contains more carbon, emissions of CO_2 from a diesel may not be much lower. NSCA leaflet *Choosing and Using a Cleaner Car* looks at the relative merits of petrol and diesel cars. Regular tuning and maintenance of any vehicle is an important factor in keeping emissions low. Vehicles are monitored for correct tuning to ensure that they continue to meet standards in the annual MOT test.

Alternative fuels – Low pollu-ting fuels offer another option. Methanol, ethanol, methane, liquid gas, hydrogen and electricity all have advantages. Some are already finding limited uses, but they tend to be expensive or present design difficulties which limit widespread use. Improvements in fuel efficiency may be achieved through better aerodynamics and the use of lighter materials.

Reducing traffic

Even if strict emission limits are achieved for all motor vehicles, the rapid growth in vehicle ownership and use means that the total amount of pollution may not be reduced much, and is predicted to continue to rise. In the UK the distance driven each year increased by 11% between 1986 and 1996. Our traditional freedom to drive where and when we like could eventually result in a worsening environment for every-one. Some countries have already taken steps to actively discourage the use of motor vehicles in particular situations.

The role of local authorities – Pedestrianisation and limiting roads to bus, taxi and cycle use are increasingly common in towns and cities. Vehicle users could be charged for entering particular zones using automatic detectors in the road which periodically bill vehicles or tolls on particular roads. Local Authorities are responsible for managing air quality in their area to ensure that health guidelines are not exceeded. Under the Environment Act 1995, they may soon be able to restrict traffic and stop and fine polluting vehicles in order to control pollution. Tax incentives, high car-parking fees and strict enforcement of parking restrictions can also discourage private car use. In the US, many companies operate car pools or car-sharing schemes.

Public transport – Most cities in the world operate a subsidised public transport system. Some have incentives for employers to give public transport passes to employees.

Cycling – In 1986 bicycles were used to cover 5.5 billion kilometres, causing no pollution at all. By 1996 this had reduced to 4.3 billion. In 1996 the Department of Transport published a National Cycling Strategy to encourage cycle use – many local authorities and some employers are considering ways of doing this.

Driver behaviour – When considering long-range pollution such as photochemical smog and acid rain, driver behaviour is an important factor. High-speed motoring increases NOx emissions – enforcing speed limits would reduce emissions and fuel consumption. Slow stop-start driving increases HC emissions. In towns, unnecessary pollution is caused by stationary vehicles; some European cities insist that drivers turn off their engines whilst waiting at traffic lights. Finally, aggressive driving – unnecessary acceleration and revving – wastes fuel, increases pollution and noise.

Financial measures – An environment tax on fuels would encourage energy conservation. Financial measures favouring the use of public transport could also be employed. Since the early 1980s some European countries have offered tax incentives to drivers buying less-polluting vehicles. These have included diesels and petrol-engined cars fitted with catalysts. Limiting the use of large-engined cars, either absolutely or by financial disincentives, will help reduce emissions. In the UK unleaded petrol, ultra low sulphur diesel, gas fuels and low-emission lorries are subsidised.

Planning for pollution

Planners and architects can help reduce traffic pollution. Designing roads and traffic management systems which ease congestion and keep traffic flowing at a steady speed will reduce air pollution and noise. Streets with high buildings on both sides create a 'canyon' effect, trapping pollutants. An alternating profile of low and high buildings increases air turbulence and improves street ventilation.

Building design can do much to reduce the effects of traffic noise. Where new roads are built or existing roads upgraded, householders qualify for sound insulation grants. However, where noise is the result of gradually increasing traffic on existing roads, grants are discretionary and rarely available. Road design and the use of barriers can reduce traffic noise at source.

Building roads to alleviate traffic congestion does not recognise the rise in pollution levels that an increase in motor vehicle use brings, or the inefficient use of land and resources that such a policy represents. Policies must be devised which discourage the unnecessary use of road vehicles and present viable alternatives. Increased public awareness of the environmental impact of road traffic will be necessary if this is to become politically acceptable.

© NSCA October 1999

Safe Routes to Schools

Information from Sustrans

Safe Routes to Schools is a concept promoted by Sustrans and supported by central and local government. The aims are to enable more children to walk and cycle to school. This is done by making changes to the highway, principally reducing traffic speeds and volumes and reallocating road space; and by raising awareness of transport, sustainability and health. Safe Routes to Schools projects are co-operative ventures between local authorities, school staff and students, parents, and local residents.

The 1998 Government White Paper, *A New Deal for Transport: Better for Everyone*, provides extensive support for Safe Routes to Schools and says: 'We will work with local councils to make walking safer and to provide more cycle routes to schools. Schools will be encouraged to improve facilities for cyclists'.[1]

This information explains the background to Safe Routes to School, who is involved, what can be done to support local projects, and gives further sources of information.

Why do we need Safe Routes to Schools?

There are many benefits from setting up a Safe Routes to Schools project:
- to reduce traffic congestion and pollution
- to improve safety
- to benefit our children's health
- to encourage children's confidence and independence
- to reduce parental time escorting children.

Reducing traffic congestion and pollution

Traffic is increasing all the time, leading to more congestion and pollution. Road traffic volumes have nearly doubled over the last two decades, and the Department of the Environment, Transport and the Regions (DETR) forecasts that over the next 20 years traffic could grow by more than a third.[2]

In urban areas, up to one in five cars on the road during peak traffic periods is being used to drive a child to school,[3] even though for two-thirds of all children the journey to school is less than 2 miles.[4] The number of children being driven to school is increasing year on year. Four times as many English children are collected by car from school than in Germany.[5] The proportion of children travelling to school by car has risen from 16% in 1985/86 to 29% in 1995/97.[6]

Parents who drive their children to school are not only adding to traffic congestion, but are unknowingly exposing their children to high levels of pollution. Motorists and their passengers are at most risk from exhaust fumes. Car passengers in slow-moving traffic face pollution levels inside a car two to three times higher than those experienced by pedestrians, so children inside cars can suffer more than those outside.[7]

Children themselves care passionately about the environment. The Children's Parliament on the Environment is asking the Government to 'Ensure that we have clean air to breathe through a combination of measures including: a transport policy which will reduce the number of cars and lorries on the roads and encourage greater use of public transport and walking'.[8]

Improving safety

The amount of traffic on our roads makes them dangerous places, and this is the reason why many parents feel they need to drive their children to school. The Government, however, sees the need to improve safety as an incentive for creating safer cycling and walking conditions, rather than a reason for delaying action.[9]

A cyclist venturing out on British roads is more likely to be killed or injured than their counterpart in Denmark, the Netherlands or Sweden, where there is a higher percentage of car ownership than in Britain. The cyclist casualty rate, per distance travelled, in Great Britain

is more than 10 times as high as in The Netherlands.[10]

In the early 1970s Denmark had the highest rate of child mortality from traffic accidents in Western Europe. In 1976, legislation was introduced to protect children from the danger of motor traffic on their way to and from school and a pilot project installing safe routes to schools was established in Odense. As a result, over 10 years, child pedestrian and cycle casualties have been cut by 80%.

18% of all journeys in Denmark are now made by bike, and more than 60% of young people cycle to school.[11] This compares to under 3% of all journeys made by bike in Britain, with just 1% of school children cycling to school.[12]

Benefiting children's health and fitness

Most children are not physically active enough and this is damaging their health. A survey for the Chartered Society of Physiotherapy found that 'many of today's children lack stamina; are short of breath after the simplest exercise; have poor posture leading to lower back pain; are tired and lethargic'.[13]

Health professionals agree that patterns of physical activity need to be established in childhood, as sedentary children are more likely to become sedentary and unhealthy adults. Physical activity in adults is recognised as having many benefits in reducing illness and premature death from conditions such as coronary heart disease, diabetes, high blood pressure, obesity and osteo-porosis.[14]

Rising obesity amongst British children is a cause for concern. The rise in obesity mirrors the trend in car-dependent USA, where obesity affects one in five children.[15]

Not only are walking and cycling both excellent forms of physical activity, they are accessible to most people, affordable and can be integrated into daily travel patterns with no special facilities – apart from safe streets.

The Health Education Authority, the British Medical Association and the Institute of Child Health, University College of London, have all recognised that driving children to school is starving them of exercise. They all conclude that improving road safety conditions will make a significant contribution to improving the nation's health through more people taking more exercise.[16]

Encouraging children's confidence and independence

A knock-on effect of fears for our children's safety is the increase in parental supervision. Only one children in nine aged 10 or younger travels to school unaccompanied, compared to one in five ten years ago.[17]

Fears about personal safety have increased, although there is no evidence that the actual risk of abduction or assault has increased. Home Office figures show that an average of between 6 and 7 children were killed by strangers each year between 1985 and 1994, and whilst the numbers vary year on year, the statistics have shown no increasing trend[18]. This is covered in more detail in a separate information sheet, *Safety on the Streets for Children*.[19]

The Suzy Lamplugh Trust, which provides advice on personal safety, urges parents to use the school journey as an opportunity for parents to teach safety skills to children. Their advice is: 'Children must be allowed to learn that they do have intuition, that they can use to stay safe. Personal and road safety skills will help children to recognise and avoid potential problems, and to cope if things do go wrong'.[20]

Children are generally aware of their parents' concerns and this can increase their own worries about the world beyond the home, under-mining their confidence.[21] Travelling everywhere by car establishes car dependency at an early age in a child's development and reduces children's knowledge of their neighbourhood.

The Government's White Paper, *Our Healthier Nation*, warns that 'in using private cars more we are restricting not only children's physical well-being but also their social development. Unless they have a chance to learn early on how to make decisions for themselves, children may eventually be at more risk on the roads and in other public places'.[22] The British Medical Association has even warned that there could be some effects on children's mental development.[23]

Walking and cycling to school are good ways for children to gain confidence and make friends, and most often these are the ways children would prefer to get to school if they were given the choice.[24]

Reducing parental time escorting children

Partly in response to increasing road dangers, the escorting responsibilities of parents have risen markedly. Over half of British parents now escort their children to school and elsewhere, and the average mother of two or more young children devotes nearly one hour of each working day to this.[25]

If parents knew that their children's journey to school was safe they would be encouraged to allow them to walk or cycle, for example with friends or through 'Walking Bus' schemes. This would free up more of their own time.

The National Cycle Network and School Links

Sustrans is co-ordinating the development of the National Cycle Network, a linked series of traffic-free paths and traffic-calmed roads providing 9,000 miles of safe and attractive routes all over the country by 2005. By opening up opportunities for people to cycle more, the Network will help create a culture that welcomes cycling as an activity.

During the last twenty years, Sustrans has built many miles of traffic-free paths in urban areas throughout Britain. These are sited to link with as many schools and amenities for young people as possible, and to link these with the countryside.

These routes are heavily used by children for both school and out-of-school trips, and demonstrate just how many children will choose to walk and cycle as long as the conditions are made safe and attractive.

Sustrans has assisted local authorities throughout the UK to identify schools which are close to the National Cycle Network and which would benefit by being linked to it, and provided support for the creation of a link using Millennium Commission grant funds.

Further information
The Safe Routes to Schools project co-ordinated by Sustrans provides support to local authorities, schools and parents. It publishes a quarterly newsletter, teachers' packs, project guides and information sheets, organises conferences and seminars, and provides a helpline for enquiries.

Sustrans is a member of the School Travel Advisory Group and has contributed to the best practice guide on School Travel Strategies and Plans published by the DETR

References
1 *A New Deal for Transport: Better for Everyone*, Transport White Paper, DETR, 1998.
2 *ibid*
3 *National Travel Survey 1994/96*, Transport Statistics Report, DETR, 1997.
4 *Travel to School*, Personal Travel Factsheet 2, DETR, June 1999.
5 *One False Move . . . a study of Children's Independent Mobility*. Mayer Hillman, John Adams and John Whitelegg. Policy Studies Institute, 1990.
6 *National Travel Survey 1995/97*, Transport Statistics Report, DETR, 1998. The figures quoted at 95/97 are an average of the years 1995-1997.
7 *Comparative Pollution Exposure of Road Users*, Environmental Transport Association Trust, 1997.
8 *Action Plan to Prime Minister*, Children's Parliament on the Environment, press release 25 May 1999.
9 as 1 above.
10 Cycling in Safety?, from *Safety 1991 Proceedings*, J.M. Morgan, Transport Research Laboratory.
11 *1996 National Cycling Strategy*, Department of Transport.
12 *Travel to School*, Personal Travel Factsheet 2, DETR, June 1999. NB. 2% of secondary school children (11-16) cycle to school and the figure for primary age children (5-10) is negligible.
13 Physiotherapists concerned about unfit, fat, flabby young people, Chartered Society of Physiotherapy, Press Release June 26th 1995.
14 *The School Run – Blessing or Blight?* Institute of Child Health & Pedestrians' Association, 1998.
15 *ibid*
16 *Active Living*, Active Recreation & Sports, Health Education Authority, 1992; *Cycling: Towards Health and Safety*, British Medical Association, 1992; *The School Run – Blessing or Blight?* Institute of Child Health & Pedestrians' Association, 1998.
17 *National Travel Survey 1994/96*, Transport Statistics Report, DETR, 1997.
18 *Criminal Statistics England and Wales 1994*, Home Office, HMSO, 1995; *Transport Statistics Great Britain*, Department of Transport, HMSO, 1995; *Road Accidents in Great Britain*, Department of Transport, HMSO, 1995.
19 *Safety on the Streets for Children*, Sustrans Information Sheet FS02, 1996.
20 *Better Ways to School Newsletter*, Oxfordshire County Council Environmental Services, June 1998.
21 *Safety on the Streets for Children*, Sustrans Information Sheet FS02, 1996.
22 as 19 above
23 *Road Transport and Health*, British Medical Association, 1997.
24 Safe Routes to Schools Project – Findings of Schools Survey, Sustrans, 1996.
25 *Children. Transport and Quality of Life* – conference by Johnathan Gershuny, edited by Mayer Hillman, PSI, 1993.

• The above information is an extract from the Sustrans information sheet *Safe Routes to Schools*, produced by Sustrans. See page 41 for address details.

© Sustrans

Ten facts about children and roads

1. Two-thirds of all fatal accidents involving school-aged children are the result of road accidents.

2. In 1996 over 40,000 children were killed or injured on our roads. Of these, around 37,000 were pedestrians and cyclists.

3. Most child pedestrian accidents happen close to home, on residential roads.

4. Accidents peak between eight and nine o'clock in the morning, and between three and six o'clock in the afternoon, as children travel to and from school.

5. More children are knocked down in summer, when they spend time playing outside without supervision.

6. The most dangerous age for children is between twelve and fifteen.

7. In a recent survey, parents of primary school children said road accidents were the most worrying threat to their children. Parents of secondary school children were more worried about drugs.

8. 20mph zones can reduce accidents involving child pedestrians and cyclists by around 70%

9. Severity of injury is closely linked to speed. Hit at 20mph one pedestrian in twenty is killed, while at 40mph only one in ten survives.

10. Drivers can make the most difference in reducing road accidents by slowing down, especially when children are around.

© Department of the Environment, Transport and the Regions

Parking ban demanded to halt school run chaos

By Liz Lightfoot,
Education Correspondent

Teachers called yesterday for no-parking zones within a quarter-mile radius of schools to ease the chaos of the school run.

Restrictions at peak times would encourage parents to walk their children to school or use public transport, members of the Professional Association of Teachers suggested. Parents taking their children to school or picking them up account for a million car journeys a day, or one in five during rush-hour traffic.

Although the Government has urged parents to share cars or organise supervised walks, members of the 35,000-member union decided that firmer action was needed to change the driving habit. Wesley Paxton, from Hull, said that parents' addiction to cars amounted to 'auto-holism'. This damaged young children, who grew up expecting to be driven everywhere.

Mr Paxton told the union's annual conference in Southport, Merseyside: 'Children need the exercise of walking or biking to school. They need to learn to use roads without them being like a grand prix circuit at school time. Above all, they need to learn the independence of getting about on their own.'

Car exhausts exacerbated asthma, which was increasing among children, Mr Paxton said. Despite parental paranoia, child abductions and murders by strangers were rare. He added: 'But today road vehicles will kill four people walking or biking and another six inside the vehicles.'

Jane Hetherington, who represents the West Midlands on the union's ruling council, said that traffic wardens with cameras could be used to enforce the no-parking zones. Many parents drove their children to school in urban areas, although they lived only half a mile away, she said.

Kathleen Barraclough, a head teacher from Surrey, said that her time was taken up on many mornings dealing with calls from irate residents whose drives had been blocked by parents' cars. She said: 'However, I urge caution, because there is a bigger picture.

'There are areas where it is not safe for our children to walk because of gangs. My administrator's daughter has been thoroughly intimidated outside the school in a relatively safe area. Then there are lonely country lanes which may not be the best places for children to walk.' Parents also feared racist attacks and drugs outside the gates of some schools, she said.

Charles Clarke, the junior education minister, angered the teachers earlier when he refused to rule out the use of pupils' exam and test results as part of the new performance-related pay system.

He said: 'Teachers can and do make a difference. We cannot have a system which fails to recognise the contribution teachers make to their pupils' achievement. This is not a crude system of payment by results; it is about how well teachers help their pupils progress from one stage of learning to another.'

Under the Government's plans, teachers will be able to earn extra if they agree to be assessed as good enough to go through a threshold to reach a new higher salary scale. Teachers earning around £23,500 when they go through the threshold will receive an initial £2,000 and prospects of further increases and salaries of up to £35,000.

The teaching unions have opposed the suggestion in the Government's consultation paper that pupils' test and examination results might be taken into account when assessing a teacher's performance. Mr Clarke announced that the Government was to give schools £22 million over three years to help them develop teacher appraisal systems.

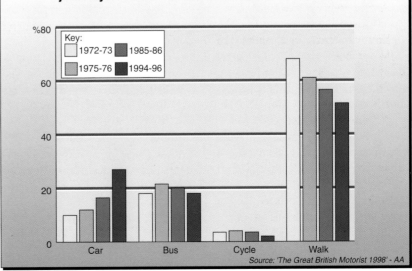

Journeys to school by main means of travel

In the 1960s many more children walked or cycled to school, and went to school unescorted, than in the 1990s. Walking is still the most common means of travel to school, but car journeys almost trebled between 1972 and 1994.

Key:
- 1972-73
- 1975-76
- 1985-86
- 1994-96

Source: 'The Great British Motorist 1998' - AA

The evolution of Reclaim the Streets

The direct action group Reclaim the Streets (RTS) has developed widespread recognition over the last few years. From road blockades to street parties, from strikes on oil corporations to organising alongside striking workers, its actions and ideas are attracting more and more people and international attention. Yet the apparent sudden emergence of this group, its penetration of popular alternative culture and its underlying philosophy have rarely been discussed.

RTS was originally formed in London in autumn 1991, around the dawn of the anti-roads movement. With the battle for Twyford Down rumbling along in the background, a small group of individuals got together to undertake direct action against the motor car. In their own words they were campaigning: 'For walking, cycling and cheap, or free, public transport, and against cars, roads and the system that pushes them.'[1]

Their work was small-scale but effective and even back then it had elements of the cheeky, surprise tactics which have moulded RTS's more recent activities. There was the trashed car on Park Lane symbolising the arrival of Carmageddon, DIY cycle lanes painted overnight on London streets, disruption of the 1993 Earls Court Motor Show and subvertising actions on car adverts around the city. However the onset of the No M11 Link Road Campaign presented the group with a specific local focus, and RTS was absorbed temporarily into the No M11 campaign in East London.

This period of the No M11 Campaign was significant for a number of reasons. Whilst Twyford Down was predominantly an ecological campaign – defending a 'natural' area – the urban setting of the resistance to the M11 construction embodied wider social and political issues. Beyond the anti-road and ecological arguments, a whole urban community faced the destruction of its social environment with loss of homes, degradation to its quality of life and community fragmentation.

Beyond these political and social considerations, the M11 campaign developed the direct action skills of those involved. Phone trees were established, large numbers of people were involved in site invasions, crowds of activists had to be manoeuvred cunningly to outwit police. The protesters also gained experience of dealing with associated tasks such as publicity, the media and fund-raising.

Then in late 1994 a political hand-grenade was thrown into the arena of the M11 campaign: the Criminal Justice and Public Order Act. Overnight civil protesting became a criminal act, but what the government hadn't counted on was how this piece of legislation would unite and motivate the very groups it was aimed at repressing. The fight of the anti-road activists became synonymous with that of travellers, squatters and hunt saboteurs. In particular, the suddenly politicised rave scene became a communal social focus for many people.

The No M11 Link Road campaign culminated in the symbolic and dramatic battle of Claremont Road. Eventually, and with the repetitive beats of The Prodigy in the background, police and security overpowered the barricades, lock-ons and the scaffold tower, but the war was only just beginning. The period of the M11 Campaign had linked together new political and social alliances and in the midst of the campaign's frenzied activities strong friendships had been formed. When Claremont Road was lost, this collective looked for new sources of expression and Reclaim the Streets was reformed in February 1995.

The years that followed saw the momentum of RTS flourish. Street Parties I and II were held in rapid succession in the summer of 1995 and there were various actions against the likes of Shell, the Nigerian Embassy and the 1995 Motor Show. More recently, in July 1996 there was the massive success of the M41 Street Party, where for nine hours 8,000 people took control of the M41 motorway in West London and partied and enjoyed themselves, whilst some dug up the tarmac with jack-hammers and in its place planted trees that had been rescued from the construction path of the M11.

At a base level the focus of RTS has remained anti-car but this has been increasingly symbolic, not specific. RTS aimed initially to move debate beyond the anti-roads struggle, to highlight the social, as well as the ecological, costs of the car system: 'The cars that fill the streets have narrowed the pavements . . . [If] pedestrians . . . want to look at each other, they see cars in the background, if they want to look at the building across the street they see cars in the foreground: there isn't a single angle of view from which cars will not be visible, from the back, in front, on both sides. Their omnipresent noise corrodes every moment of contemplation like acid.'[2]

Cars dominate our cities, polluting, congesting and dividing communities. They have isolated people from one another, and our streets have become mere conduits for motor vehicles to hurtle through, oblivious of the neighbourhoods they are disrupting. Cars have created social voids; allowing people to move further and further away from their homes, dispersing and fragmenting daily activities and lives and increasing social anonymity. RTS believe that ridding society of the car would allow us to re-create a safer, more attractive living environment, to return streets to the people that live on them and perhaps to rediscover a sense of 'social solidarity'.

But cars are just one piece of the jigsaw and RTS is also about raising the wider questions behind the transport issue – about the political and economic forces which drive 'car culture'. Governments claim that 'roads are good for the economy'. More goods travelling on longer journeys, more petrol being burnt, more customers at out-of-town supermarkets – it is all about increasing 'consumption', because that is an indicator of 'economic growth'. The greedy, short-term exploitation of dwindling resources regardless of the immediate or long-term costs. Therefore RTS's attack on cars cannot be detached from a wider attack on capitalism itself.

'Our streets are as full of capitalism as of cars and the pollution of capitalism is much more insidious.'[3]

More importantly, RTS is about encouraging more people to take part in direct action. Everyone knows the destruction which roads and cars are causing, yet the politicians still take no notice. Hardly surprising – they only care about staying in power and maintaining their 'authority' over the majority of people. Direct action is about destroying that power and authority, and people taking responsibility for themselves. Direct action is not just a tactic; it is an end in itself. It is about enabling people to unite as individuals with a common aim, to change things directly by their own actions.

Street Parties I, II and III were an ingenious manifestation of RTS's views. They embodied the above messages in an inspired formula: cunning direct action, crowd empowerment, fun, humour and raving. They have evolved into festivals open to all who feel exasperated by conventional society.

To some extent it is possible to trace the tactics behind the Street Parties in RTS's history. The mobilisation, assembly and movement of large crowds draws on skills from road protests. The use of sound systems draws on dominant popular culture whereas the initial inspiration for

Street Parties certainly reflects the parties of the Claremont Road days. However, RTS have retrospectively also realised that their roots lie deeper in history. The great revolutionary moments have all been enormous popular festivals – the storming of the Bastille, the Paris commune and the uprisings in 1968 to name a few. A carnival celebrates temporary liberation from the established order; it marks the suspension of all hierarchy, rank, privileges, norms and prohibitions. Crowds of people on the street seized by a sudden awareness of their power and unification through a celebration of their own ideas and creations. It follows then that carnivals and revolutions are not spectacles seen by other people, but the very opposite in that they involve the active participation of the crowd itself. Their very idea embraces all people, and the Street Party as an event has successfully harnessed this emotion.

The power which such activities embody inevitably challenges the state's authority, and hence the police and security services' attention has increasingly been drawn to RTS. The organisation of any form of direct action by the group is closely scrutinised. RTS has been made very aware of this problem. Vehicles carrying equipment have been broken into, followed and impounded *en route* to Street Parties, RTS's office has been raided, telephones have been bugged and activists from RTS have been followed, harassed and threatened with heavy conspiracy charges. On top of this a secret RTS action in December 1996 (an attempt to seize a BP tanker on the M25) was foiled

by the unexpected presence of two hundred police at the activists' meeting point. How such information is obtained by the police is uncertain and can easily lead to paranoia in the group; fear of infiltration, anxiety and suspicion which can themselves be debilitating.

Yet RTS has not been deterred, they hold open meetings every week, they continue to expand and involve new people, and are also frequently approached by other direct action groups. Alliances have sprouted with other groups – the striking Liverpool Dockers and Tube Workers to name two – as recognition has grown of common ground between these struggles. Throughout the UK and Europe new local RTS groups have formed and late this summer there are likely to be Street Parties worldwide. These new groups have not been created by London RTS, they are fully autonomous. London RTS has merely acted as a catalyst; stimulating individuals to replicate ideas if they are suitable for others to use as well.

In many ways the evolution of RTS has been a logical progression which reflects its roots and experiences. Equally the forms of expression which RTS have adopted are merely modern interpretations of age-old protests: direct action is not a new invention. Like their historic revolutionary counterparts, they are a group fighting for a better society at a time when many people feel alienated from, and concerned about, the current system. Their success lies in their ingenuity for empowering people, their foresight to forge common ground between issues and their ability to inspire.

References
1. Reclaim The Streets leaflet.
2. *Immortality*, Milan Kundera (Faber and Faber: London 1991) – page 271.
3. *Reclaim The Streets Agit-Prop* (Distributed at the M41 Street Party on Saturday 13th July 1996).

• The above information is an extract from the Reclaim the Streets web site which can be found at www.gn.apc.org/rts/
© *Reclaim the Streets (RTS)*

Fair deal?

Tax

- In every £10 spent on fuel £8.50 is tax.
- 72 per cent of motorists say the level of tax on fuel is unacceptable.
- In every £8 of road-user tax, only £1.50 is spent on roads and local public transport.
- In 1997-98 the government took £31 billion in tax from road users but less than £6 billion went back into roads and local public transport.
- 82 per cent of motorists say it is unacceptable that so little of their motoring taxes is spent on roads and public transport.
- Fuel prices have risen by more than 50 per cent since 1992 – while spending on roads and local public transport has fallen by 23 per cent.
- Petrol and diesel in the UK is the most expensive anywhere in Europe.
- If the Chancellor continues to increase tax as he plans, within five years a litre will be 80p (at today's prices) of which 70p will be tax.
- Increasing fuel tax hits vulnerable and less well-off families.
- The government plans new charges on motorists – charges to park at work, tolls to drive in towns and tolls on motorways – on top of existing motoring taxes.
- Motorists do not accept the current balance of tax and spend. The highest fuel tax in Europe must be matched by investment to give Britain a world-class road and transport system.

Spend

- Britain's transport investment is half the typical European level and our road congestion the worst.
- Current annual investment in road and local public transport is less than £6 billion.
- The road maintenance backlog on local roads alone is £5 billion.
- The road maintenance bill is rising by £1 billion each year for want of 'stitch in time' maintenance.
- Britain's lamp posts will have to last for more than 100 years at current levels of replacement.
- Roads which are laid out to modern safety standards are twice as safe.
- NHS wards deal with wholly avoidable casualties because blackspots are not treated and white lines, road surfaces and traffic signs are worn out.
- The UK has 500 bypasses outstanding – many communities suffering from heavy through traffic have been waiting for more than 50 years for their bypass.
- Britain's environmental engineering is cheap and nasty – flimsy noise barriers, noisy road surfaces, and scars through landscapes where tunnels should have been built.

© The Automobile Association, Group Public Policy Department

Councils 'waste millions' on public transport

By Paul Marston, Transport Correspondent

Local councils may be wasting hundreds of millions of pounds subsidising bus and rail services that are unreliable, inconvenient and a poor alternative to the car, a recent Audit Commission report said.

Councils spent £1 billion a year on supporting public transport. Yet monitoring of sponsored routes was 'often neither comprehensive nor robust'. Public transport was generally held in low esteem, with many passengers choosing it as a last resort. While 90 per cent of motorists chose their form of transport, that was true for only 29 per cent of bus passengers. Buses and trains were widely regarded as unpunctual, expensive and unsafe. A fifth of elderly people said they were difficult to use.

Yet despite their unpopularity, the main bus operators enjoyed strong profits of nine per cent and were protected from competition. Large-scale subsidies were handed to transport companies 'without, in many cases, clear objectives or adequate monitoring'. Spending per head varied from almost £100 to less than £10. Some bus routes were subsidised on the basis of 'outdated information' while eligibility for concessionary fares and door-to-door bus schemes varied widely and were 'not based on what people need'.

A significant proportion of routes typically carried fewer than five passengers at any one time. One transport officer had said: 'I sometimes think it would be cheaper to pay for a taxi to run up and down that road and let people get on and off whenever they wanted.' Councils needed to compare information on spending per head, subsidy per mile and cost per trip of door-to-door services.

The officer said: 'Councillors need to confront the reality that making buses and trains safer, cleaner and more reliable will not be enough to secure the shift away from the car. Coercive measures are also required.' These could include rigorous enforcement of an expanded bus lane network, workplace parking charges and road tolls.

End of the road for park and ride?

Far from easing congestion and pollution in our cities, evidence suggests that taking drivers into town by bus only makes matters worse. Andrew Baxter reports

Government-funded park-and-ride services aimed at persuading motorists to take the bus only add to congestion and pollution, according to a new survey.

The report, by the University College of London's influential Transport Studies Unit, comes in the wake of mounting concerns about unsightly car parks springing up on green-belt land and fears that they attract car thieves. And it flies in the face of research by the Department of the Environment, Transport and the Regions which concluded that park-and-ride schemes reduce road hold-ups and benefit the environment.

Author Dr Graham Parkhurst said the DETR got its sums wrong by failing to take account of the extra car journeys to park-and-ride sites by people who previously used buses within walking distance of their homes. Subsequent questionnaires revealed they are attracted by the fast and frequent – and often cheaper – bus services from edge-of-town termini where parking is usually free.

The combined effect of people making additional car journeys and the extra buses laid on to take them into town means that the total mileage covered by vehicles overall actually increases.

'It seems common sense that if you provide one standard of service for car drivers and a lower standard for bus users then it'll only be a matter of time before bus users switch to park and ride,' said Dr Parkhurst. 'Park and ride is often actually cheaper and quicker than taking the bus all the way from near people's homes.'

'Although park and ride gets motorists out of their cars in town centres, people get into their cars to reach the park-and-ride starting point in the first place'

Dr Parkhurst based his findings on DETR figures for schemes in Brighton, Cambridge, Coventry, Norwich, Plymouth, Reading, Shrewsbury and York, which transport minister Glenda Jackson claimed 'dispelled the myth that park and ride results in a net increase in car mileage'.

The DETR insisted that each car left at park-and-ride facilities would travel two and a half miles less each day on average.

But Dr Parkhurst calculated that there was a net increase in overall vehicle mileage per car in Cambridge, Coventry and Norwich once the effect of extra bus services was taken into account. In Coventry, the rise was 1.1 miles per car while the increase was 0.64 miles in Cambridge and 0.14 miles in Norwich.

He also estimated the reductions in the remaining five would be outweighed once the extra mileage of passengers who previously used other forms of public transport was added into the equation.

The DETR statistics contained in a report entitled *The Travel Effects of Park and Ride* suggest that up to two-thirds of those parking at 19 sites in the eight towns and cities previously drove into the city centre. But as many as 28 per cent of passengers surveyed said they were lured from

other public transport services and around half of these previously walked or cycled to their nearest bus stop or train station.

Dr Parkhurst, a research fellow at the unit funded by the Economic Social Research Council, said park-and-ride buses frequently run empty during the day once car parks are full of commuters' cars.

'Most park-and-ride users tend to be commuters, so the car parks fill up before nine o'clock in the morning. If shoppers want to use the service later in the day they often can't find a space to park,' he said.

The environmental effect is particularly significant because buses typically run every 10 minutes between 7am and 7pm and produce up to three times as much pollution as cars.

Dr Parkhurst estimates that in Cambridge, which has four park-and-ride sites, buses cause more pollution and environmental damage than is gained by the reduction in inner-city private car mileage.

His report, *Environmental Cost Benefits of Bus-Based Park-and-Ride Schemes*, is bound to compound concerns raised by the World Health Organisation, which claims traffic fumes kill more people than road crashes.

Environmental groups such as the Council for the Protection of Rural England also oppose park-and-ride schemes because they fear huge swathes of open fields will disappear as more terminals spring up on the edge of towns.

The development of one site at Oxford – the first city to introduce a scheme, in 1973 – was recently halted after a public inquiry and there is an outcry in Winchester where the city and county councils face a High Court bid to block plans to turn a nature reserve into a car park.

Lilli Matson, head of transport at the CPRE, said: 'There has been an explosion of park-and-ride schemes in recent years. Ever since the deregulation of buses, local authorities have been unable to put money into services but have received government funds to subsidise park and ride.' In the past 12 months, 65 schemes have begun operating after the Government awarded councils a total of £14 million in grants.

Pressure group Transport 2000 accused the DETR of 'cooking the books' by slanting its figures in favour of park and ride. 'We are unhappy with the way the results were analysed and believe the figures show the opposite,' said spokesman Steve Hounsham.

Environmental groups oppose park-and-ride schemes because they fear huge swathes of open fields will disappear as more terminals spring up on the edge of towns

---

'Although park and ride gets motorists out of their cars in town centres, people get into their cars to reach the park-and-ride starting point in the first place. This is counter-productive. A more environmentally friendly solution is to encourage people to use public transport from their front door.'

The park-and-ride approach is in marked contrast to an innovative project in Southampton which aims to ease the flow of traffic for both private motorists and buses. Traffic and parking information is displayed on variable message signs on the city's approach roads and posted on an Internet site while digital displays at bus stops inform passengers when the next service will arrive.

'We were keen to introduce park and ride but it is a very expensive option,' said parking manager David Logan. 'To make it work you have to restrict parking in the centre of town, as they have done in Oxford and Canterbury, or make it very attractive for people to use, which would impose a huge annual cost on ratepayers.'

Dr Parkhurst believes one answer could be to run park and ride schemes from farther out of town along existing bus routes with several smaller car parks, much like train stations along a railway line. 'People are not aware of the full implications. Park-and-ride is essentially about maintaining car use rather than changing it,' said Dr Parkhurst.

• First published in *The Daily Telegraph*, July, 1999.

© *Andrew Baxter*

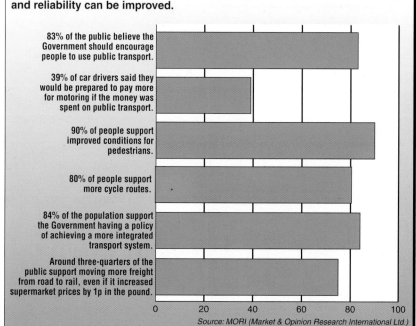

Alternatives to driving

The public will consider many alternatives to driving – if conditions are right. A national survey canvassed people's opinions on the current network and asked their views on improvements. The poll demonstrated that there is a widespread willingness to switch journeys from the car to other modes of transport – such as trains, buses, and walking – if their convenience-safety and reliability can be improved.

83% of the public believe the Government should encourage people to use public transport.

39% of car drivers said they would be prepared to pay more for motoring if the money was spent on public transport.

90% of people support improved conditions for pedestrians.

80% of people support more cycle routes.

84% of the population support the Government having a policy of achieving a more integrated transport system.

Around three-quarters of the public support moving more freight from road to rail, even if it increased supermarket prices by 1p in the pound.

Source: MORI (Market & Opinion Research International Ltd.)

All aboard for better bus and train services

Local authorities can help to improve public transport

Good public transport makes a vital contribution to the quality of life of millions of people without access to a car, such as the elderly, those on low incomes and people with disabilities. It also helps to reduce congestion by encouraging drivers to leave their cars at home. However, an Audit Commission report published today shows that many bus and train services are unreliable, unsafe and inconvenient, and offer an unattractive alternative to the car.

Although most services are privately-owned, the Government and local authorities together spend £3 billion a year to support public transport and travel. However, the report reveals a lack of confidence in local transport; the bus industry is in steady decline and town-centre congestion is worsening.

The report's findings include:

- Many people have a low opinion of public transport and use local buses and trains only when they have no other alternative. For example, 90% of drivers use their cars out of choice, whereas buses are the preferred option for only 29% of users.
- Many passengers find buses and trains unreliable, expensive, unsafe and inconvenient. In addition, one-fifth of elderly people find it difficult to get to, and then use, buses and trains. Outside London, the use of buses has halved since 1970.
- Authorities provide subsidies to help certain groups such as the elderly and people with disabilities to travel. However, the policy reasons for deciding who is subsidised, and by how much, vary considerably between

areas. Furthermore, councils are not always sure whether the subsidies are reaching the right people.

Local government can help to break out of this spiral of decline. The report calls for councils and the specialist transport authorities (covering major conurbations such as the West Midlands and Merseyside) to reassess current approaches and work towards an affordable, accessible and environmentally sustainable transport service for the future.

- Transport authorities must work in partnership with operators to ensure that the taxpayer gets value for money and the consumer gets a fair deal.
- To increase public confidence in local bus and train services,

authorities should consult more effectively about their plans with passengers *and* those who choose not to use the services at present.

- Subsidies should be targeted more effectively and then monitored to ensure they reach those who need them most.
- Public transport policies should be integrated with those for other services. For example, social services transport could be linked with dial-a-ride schemes for the frail elderly or people with disabilities.

Andrew Foster, Controller of the Audit Commission, said: 'This report shows how far local authorities need to go if they are to meet the aspirations of the recent White Paper. Many people depend on local buses or trains as their only means of transport, and it is vital that they receive a good service. At the same time, if drivers are to be persuaded to leave their cars at home then public transport must provide an attractive and efficient alternative'.

'Given the financial support it provides for public transport, local government has a vital role to play in achieving these objectives. But authorities need to modernise their existing approaches and champion the interests of passengers and potential users.'

- *All Aboard: A Review of Local Authority Transport and Travel in Urban Areas Outside London* (ISBN 1 86240 152 7) is available from Audit Commission Publications on freephone 0800 502030 priced £20

Better buses

A safer journey to school

Travelling to school by bus or coach has a better safety record than travel by car. Around a fifth of all journeys to school are made by bus, and some schools have had great success in promoting and improving bus services.

The law says . . .

Local education authorities must provide free transport for children up to the age of eight who live more than two miles away from their nearest suitable school, and for eight- to 16-year-olds who live more than three miles away. Yet, in practice, a lot of children living within the two- or three-mile limits might travel by bus to school if the right service were available.

Who can help?

To improve bus services you need to work in partnership with your local authority and public transport operators. County councils and unitary authorities have public transport co-ordinators, who can help you decide what improvements are needed, and negotiate with local operators. In a metropolitan area you should contact the marketing department of the Passenger Transport Executive or, in London, London Transport.

User-friendly information

Schools are well placed to publicise school bus services to parents and children. Timetables and leaflets can be displayed in the school foyer, and sent home on a regular basis. Timetables are often hard to understand. By involving students in the design, schools may be able to produce materials that are more readable and more appealing. It is also helpful if children can be taught how to use timetables.

Low-fare schemes

In co-operation with local bus companies and the council, some schools have negotiated low-fare deals for pupils. With the help of the school in promoting the offer, bus use picks up and can cover the cost of the discount. You may need to ask the council to underwrite any extra costs for an initial period.

Convenient times and routes

Buses may not run along the best routes or at the best times to meet pupils' needs. By working with the council and bus operators, schools have succeeded in:

- changing routes to make them more convenient
- changing times to fit with the school day
- introducing new bus services for areas poorly served by existing transport.

Your survey results and information about numbers of children coming from different areas can help in deciding what changes would be useful. Postcode maps can be overlaid with existing bus routes to identify gaps in the service. The school can then write to the parents of children living in the area to ask if they would use a new service.

Who funds?

The local authority can also help explore funding possibilities. A new service that is expected to be popular may be of interest to a commercial operator. If a service is unlikely to cover its own costs then the most probable source of funding is the local authority's passenger transport budget. In rural areas, money may be available through the Government's Rural Bus Subsidy Grant – additional money being given to councils to improve public bus services in the countryside. Funding could also come from the local education authority's school transport budget (which can be spent on services that are outside legal requirements at its own discretion) but this is rare. Another possibility, if the service is only for small numbers, is to make use of spare capacity in transport used by the health sector or social services. If all else fails, parents may be able to club together to fund their own services.

Meeting the needs of the school journey

Parents will be happier about younger children using school buses if services are geared to their needs. This could mean:

- the bus picks up and drops off at convenient points in the community rather than official bus stops
- a few parents ride as escorts and help sort out any problems that come up
- children can make their way from the bus stop to school without crossing a road
- services are extremely reliable – buses that don't come on time are likely to cause particular problems for children trying to get home after school
- the driver has a positive attitude towards children
- the bus is attractive, clean and modern.

Behaviour on board

Children's behaviour on buses can range from lively to loutish. This can obviously cause tension with drivers and other passengers, and may even lead to the withdrawal of services. Schools can keep problems in check by introducing a behaviour code for bus users. Assembling children into groups for different buses before they leave school can prevent a scramble and ensure no one gets left behind. Some bus companies have run successful sessions in schools to explain how behaviour on board affects safety. Children are encouraged to put forward their own views and help work out ground rules for using public transport.

Cooler by bus?
Bus trips rose by 100 a day following a West Sussex scheme to market school buses to young people. In a survey of 11-16-year-olds at Sackville and Imberhorne Schools in East Grinstead, students said bus fares were too expensive, bus stops too far from home and timetables hard to understand. On the basis of the findings the county council financed additional bus services. All students received an easy-to-read map and a bus card entitling them to quarter fares. Leaflets used images designed to appeal to the age group, and stressed the benefits to the planet. Steve Pennington, head of Imberhorne Lower School, says the scheme was good value for the time involved. 'Kids see the sense of it and parents are more willing to give them 20p to go on the bus than to get the car out.'

Buses for village primary
Around 50 children who used to travel by car now take the bus to Lingfield Primary School in Surrey – with a dramatic reduction in conges-tion at the school gate. Two new services were introduced following problems revealed by a survey of parents: buses ran at the wrong times, the bus stops were too far away and parents were nervous about children travelling unaccompanied. Buses, funded by the council, now meet parents' concerns. Children gather at agreed local pick-up points and a parent 'guide' is employed to ride on the bus each day.

Resource file
A briefing sheet on promoting buses to young people is available from West Sussex County Council surveyor's department, The Grange, Tower Street, Chichester, West Sussex PO19 1RH, tel 01243 777437.

© Department of the Environment, Transport and the Regions
July, 1999

Bike for your life

Information from the Bicycle Association

Cycling's good for everyone!
- It's good for you . . .
  You'll get fitter, feel better, be less stressed, and live longer.
- It's good for your community . . .
  You won't be making noise or creating stress for others.
- It's good for your environment . . .
  You won't be creating pollution and poisoning the air . . . and you'll enjoy it!

Go for the feeling good factor!
Cycling perfectly fulfils the recommendations of the Sports Council and Health Education Authority for taking regular physical activity as an essential ingredient of healthy living. Regular cycling can improve health through:

Increased fitness
Your strength, stamina, aerobic fitness and general muscle function are all improved, with little risk of over-exertion or strain to your muscles or joints. Regular physical activity also facilitates other healthy behaviour – especially diet and giving up smoking.

Lowering risk of heart attack
Your heart muscles are strengthened, resting pulse is lowered and blood fat levels reduced. People taking regular physical activity suffer far less heart disease than people who don't. Cycling is one of the best ways of keeping fit.

Shedding excess weight
By burning body fat, and raising your metabolic rate you can lose weight. If you take physical activity regularly you can enjoy a more varied diet without increasing body weight. Cycling is also a more comfortable form of physical activity for the over-weight than many other activities.

Reducing stress
Anxiety, stress and depression are all alleviated, partly due to the

---

Regular cycling will improve your fitness and can help you live a long and healthy life

---

physical activity itself, and also the sheer pleasure of riding a bike. Cycling is convenient for short journeys, and often faster across town than other forms of transport. It's an ideal means of taking physical activity throughout life, because it can be adjusted to your individual level of fitness, and form a part of your daily travelling routine.

Cycling's great for everyone
Including you! The great thing about cycling is that it doesn't have to involve strenuous physical activity. You can get fitter, going where you want to go, at your own pace, in your own time.

It fits in with your daily life
Riding a bike is quick, cheap, parking is easy and it provides real door-to-door travel. Even five half-hour rides a week will help you become fitter and feel younger. The regular physical activity can make you feel less stressed, give you more zest for life, and even make you more efficient at work. And it's fun!

You don't need special equipment

Most bikes are suitable for most types of riding. The best place to buy your bike is a specialist cycle dealer – visit two or three and discuss your requirements. Remember, price should not be your only consideration. A good quality bike and good service can get your cycling off to a flying start. If you already own a bike, but haven't used it for some time, get it serviced by a competent mechanic to ensure that it is still safe to ride. And get a good quality lock so you can park it securely.

It's so simple to get started

Make sure your bike is set up with the right saddle height and handlebar position, so you are comfortable and feel in control. Get help from a more experienced cyclist, or go to your local cycle shop for advice. Go cycling with a friend to build up confidence. You have the same rights as any other road user, but you must obey the traffic laws too, and remember your Highway Code.

Your bike can take you anywhere

Many local residential roads and country lanes have very little motor traffic. The roads on industrial estates and business parks are often deserted at weekends, and so are suitable for practice. Your council may have published maps of recommended routes. You might be able to find some traffic-free cycle paths to help you gain confidence before riding in traffic. Try the canal towpath network, or a large park where cycling is allowed, or perhaps there is a converted railway path in your area.

You can do it – anytime

But there's no time like the present! Cycling is an activity for all seasons, and in Britain's mild climate there are few days too hot or too cold to enjoy being on a bike. The activity keeps you warm anyway, and you don't need to splash out on specialist clothing.

Taking care of traffic

Cycling in traffic is not as hard as you might think. Just remember these rules:
- Look where you're going, watch out for careless road users and potholes.
- Never swerve to avoid an obstacle without making sure it's safe to do so.
- Try to anticipate what's going to happen ahead.
- Signal clearly before you change direction, and take up the correct position on the road for right turns and roundabouts.
- If you feel a junction is hazardous, get off and cross on foot.
- Wear bright clothing so that other road users can see you clearly. And *remember* you do need lights to ride at night.

Cycling towards health and safety

Cycling is healthy, both for you as an individual, and for the community you live in. That's the conclusion of the British Medical Association's report, *Cycling: Towards Health and Safety.*

Regular cycling will improve your fitness and can help you live a long and healthy life. Riding a bike can also help you maintain a healthy weight. Three-quarters of all our personal journeys are less than five miles long – that's no more than half an hour on a bike. Switching these short journeys from car to bicycle will benefit everyone in the community.

You'll be helping to cut noise, air pollution and traffic congestion. So go by cycle – you'll feel better for it!

The BMA's prescription

For a cycle-friendly future
To actively promote cycling as an environmentally-friendly means of transport and as a way of improving public health, we need to:

- encourage everyone to take up cycling
- reduce vehicle speeds in urban areas
- provide safe cycle networks
- cater for cyclists' needs fully in all road schemes
- introduce council-run bike-maintenance and safety courses
- encourage children and adults to wear helmets
- make cycle training available for all children
- integrate cycling with public transport
- develop publicity and education campaigns to improve driver awareness of cyclists and pedestrians.

Where do you go from here?

Join the Cyclists' Touring Club (CTC, 69 Meadrow, Godalming, Surrey, GU7 3HS. Tel: 01483 417 217) for a range of advice, information and services on legal, insurance, technical and touring matters. The CTC's local groups organise rides and social events, and campaign for better cycle facilities.

Contact the Cycle Campaign Network (CCN, 54-57 Allison Street, Digbeth, Birmingham, B5 5TH) for details of the nearest group lobbying for better facilities for bicycle users. The largest group is the London Cycling Campaign (LCC, 228 Great Guildford Business Square, 30 Great Guildford Street, London SE1 0HS. Tel: 0171 928 7220).

If you're interested in cycle sport, contact the British Cycling Federation (BCF, National Cycling Centre, 1 Stuart Street, Manchester, M11 4DQ. Tel: 0161 230 2301) for information about your nearest club.

Look in your local library, bookshops and cycle dealers for books with more information about cycling and cycle routes. Bicycling Books (309-311 Horn Lane, London, W3 0BU. Tel: 0181 993 3484) stocks a wide range of books which you can order by post and telephone.

The full British Medical Association report, *Cycling: Towards Health and Safety*, is published by Oxford University Press, priced £5.99, and can be obtained through any good bookshop.

© *Bicycle Association*

Health benefits

Cycling

Research suggests that regular cycling is as beneficial as any other form of physical activity in promoting health. A recent review presented an impressive range of health benefits from regular cycling. Cycling provides protection against:

- coronary heart disease
- stroke
- non insulin-dependent diabetes
- falls, fractures and injuries (through improved strength and co-ordination)
- colon cancer
- overweight, and obesity.

Cycling also promotes psychological well-being, notably self-esteem.

Everyday cycling, where the individual breathes more heavily without feeling out of breath, will benefit health. Research indicates that cyclists and pedestrians absorb lower levels of pollutants from traffic fumes than any other road users. Regular cycling, such as to and from work or school, can be an easy way to achieve the recommended 'half an hour a day' of physical activity for health.

Coronary heart disease (CHD)
The key benefit of regular cycling is likely to be the reduction of CHD, as studies suggest that regular cyclists suffer fewer than half the deaths from CHD that inactive people do. CHD is both the single largest cause of death, and the single main cause of premature death. The National Audit Office (NAO) has reported that treating CHD costs the National Health Service £500 million per annum.

Stroke
There is evidence that physical activity can protect against stroke. In 1994, 68,000 men and women died of strokes. The NAO's assessment was that treatment of stroke patients, rehabilitation and longer-term care costs the National Health Service about £1.6 billion per annum, 4.5% of its budget (NAO, 1996).

Non insulin-dependent diabetes
There is considerable evidence for a relationship between physical inactivity and non insulin-dependent diabetes (NIDDM), particularly for those men with a high risk of developing NIDDM. Those groups in the population at elevated risk of NIDDM, such as those who are overweight, have high blood pressure, or a distinct parental history, could benefit from cycling.

Falls, fractures and injuries
Improved physical fitness is associated with improved muscle strength, stability, reaction time, balance and co-ordination and perhaps with decreased numbers and severity of falls. Cycling is beneficial for joints.

Colon cancer
Data from the Office of National Statistics indicate that colon cancer is the third most common form of cancer deaths, killing 5,021 males and 5,524 females in England and Wales in 1996. Evidence strongly suggests that physical activity has a protective effect against the risk of developing colon cancer.

Overweight, and obesity
Being overweight or obese is implicated in a range of health problems, including heart disease, diabetes, and joint problems. Cycling can be an important part of a programme to reduce or control weight.

Psychological well-being
Studies have shown that regular cyclists, compared with inactive people, have improved well-being, higher self-esteem and greater confidence in their ability to perform active tasks, along with better mental functioning.

Risks associated with cycling
There are concerns that risk of injury through crashes can be a barrier to cycling. However, the British Medical Association has concluded that the benefits of cycling are likely to outweigh the loss of life through cycling accidents. Evidence from the Netherlands has demonstrated that, where an on going programme of measures is implemented to improve the traffic environment for cyclists, cycle use increases while accident rates decline.

- An extract from *Promoting Cycling: Improving Health*, published by the National Cycling Forum.

© *National Cycling Forum, April, 1999*

It's official – cycling is increasing!

The latest government statistics on cycle use show that cycling has sustained an increase in 'active cyclists' since 1993.

Year	Total sample	Active cyclists
1989	9,001	574
1990	8,592	514
1991	8,692	500
1992	8,320	482
1993	8,161	420
1994	8,190	438
1995	8,029	416
1996	7,665	414
1997	7,473	423

% of active cyclists

Year	%
1989	6.4
1990	6.0
1991	5.8
1992	5.8
1993	5.1
1994	5.3
1995	5.2
1996	5.4
1997	5.7

Source: National Travel Survey

More walking

A safer journey to school

Children's freedom and the car

While child pedestrian casualties have fallen in the last 10 years, this is probably because children are increasingly kept away from traffic. Children using roads are at their most vulnerable when they first gain their independence, but may not have the road skills to match. Overall, they are most likely to become pedestrian casualties at 11, 12 and 13 (though the chances of a boy being killed as a pedestrian also peak around the age of eight).

Pedestrian training can help children to act more safely on the roads, but no child gets it right all the time. We have to make roads safer for children, and that means slower speeds and less traffic.

Walking is such an everyday activity that it is easy to take it for granted. Yet we don't walk nearly as much as we used to – about a fifth less than 20 years ago – and the loss of this exercise is a health concern. Walking to school helps children to keep fit now, and makes it more likely that they'll stay active when they are older. Younger children who walk to school with a parent or carer have the chance to build up their road sense over time, making them better prepared for independent journeys later on.

Ticket to walk

'The children love it,' says Coreen King, a parent volunteer who regularly accompanies the walking bus to Wheatfields Junior School in St Albans. 'They all chat about what they've been up to and what they watched on telly the night before.' As an added incentive, children are given a sticker for every journey and can trade them for free goods in the school bookshop.

The walking bus

Parents may have difficulty in finding time to walk to school. One option is to arrange an escort rota – so that two or three families take turns in accompanying children. Some primary schools have taken this idea much further by setting up a 'walking bus'. This is a group of children, walking to school with two parent volunteers – a 'driver', who leads the way, and a 'conductor' at the rear. The walking bus follows a set route, stopping at agreed pick-up points in the neighbourhood. Volunteers and children are kitted out with reflective clothing and a trolley can be used to carry bags. A number of safety checks are used in setting up schemes, for example:

- volunteers receive training in road safety and follow a route worked out by a road safety officer
- a ratio of at least one volunteer to eight children is recommended for junior age children
- parents sign a consent form and make sure their child understands a set of road safety guidelines
- volunteers are vetted by police to check they have no criminal background

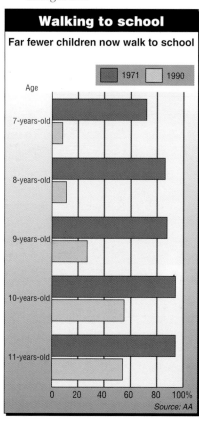

Walking to school

Far fewer children now walk to school

1971 1990

Age

7-years-old

8-years-old

9-years-old

10-years-old

11-years-old

0   20   40   60   80   100%

Source: AA

- arrangements are made for volunteers to be covered by third party public liability insurance, for example through the local authority.

Full guidelines for setting up a walking bus are available (see Resource file).

Walk to school events

Many schools promote walking by taking part in national Walk to School Week when parents are encouraged to accompany their children on foot. Badges, stickers and other materials are available (see Resource file). Some schools have gone on to run year-round campaigns for parents and children to 'walk a day a week'.

Pedestrian training

You can work with local authority road safety officers to provide practical pedestrian training for children as part of Personal, Social and Health Education. Effective training involves sessions at the roadside, rather than being purely classroom based. Many schemes train parent volunteers to work with pupils. It's important to convey to parents that children who have completed a series of sessions are not automatically 'roadworthy'. Pedestrian training should be a long-term process with frequent, short sessions at different ages. There is a particular need to raise children's awareness about road safety as they approach secondary transfer. At this age, many children gain their independence and start to make longer journeys.

Feet first

At Waingel Copse School in Reading drivers leaving the school grounds are held back for 15 minutes at the end of the day until pedestrians and cyclists have left the site.

Traffic-free entrances

Children need to be able to walk safely into school without having to weave between vehicles coming in or out. Ideally there should be a separate, traffic-free entrance for walkers and cyclists. Where pedestrians and cyclists are using the same pathway, the space should be clearly divided. Entrances should be wide enough for several people to use them at once. Even without a separate entrance, arrangements at the end of the school day can prevent a free-for-all. One idea is to hold traffic back until children who are walking or cycling have left in safety.

Visible school clothing

School uniforms are often quite dark, making it difficult for children to be seen by drivers. Consider whether changes are needed. Some schools supply reflective badges and other accessories to children at discounted prices.

Storage space

Children may be coming by car because they have to carry heavy books, musical instruments or materials for classes. Providing plenty of locker space at school can reduce the amount they need to take home and make it easier to store coats and outdoor shoes. Think about whether changes can be made to the home-

work timetable to ensure that children don't have too much to carry on any one night.

Lollipop crossings

Schools can approach the local authority road safety department to request a school crossing patrol at a busy crossing point. The decision to provide a patrol will depend on the volume of traffic and the number of unaccompanied children using the crossing. If the council refuses a permanent patrol, they may agree to provide a temporary one, and see if the numbers using the crossing point increase over time. Schools can help with recruitment, which can be difficult.

Resource file

Guidelines for setting up a walking bus are available from Environment Department, Hertfordshire County Council, County Hall, Pegs Lane, Hertford, SG13 8DN, tel 01992 555265, price £5.

ROSALIND is a computerised database of road safety education resources, for use by road safety practitioners, teachers and other professionals. Copies are available from the British Institute for Traffic

Education Research, Kent House, Kent Street, Birmingham B5 6QF, tel 0121 622 2402, price £49.95. Most road safety departments have copies they can lend to schools.

Kerbcraft, by Strathclyde University, published by the Department of the Environment, Transport and the Regions, is a resource for practical pedestrian training, available on the DETR website: www.detr.gov.uk.

Footsteps, a traffic awareness programme, is available from Oxfordshire County Council, Environmental Services, Road Safety/TravelWise Group, Speedwell House, Speedwell Street, Oxford OX1 1NE, tel 01865 815657, sample pack price £2.60.

Walk to School information packs, stickers and posters are available from the Pedestrians Association, 31-33 Bondway, Vauxhall, London SW8 1SJ, tel 0171 820 1010 or 020 7820 1010, price £5 for pack. Other Walk to School resources are available from National TravelWise Association, contact John Sykes at Hertfordshire County Council on 01992 556117.

© Department of the Environment, Transport and the Regions July, 1999

When walking do you suffer road rage?

Information from the Pedestrians Association

We are all pedestrians, even if we own a car. Nearly all journeys involve a walk but all too often the things that make walking a more pleasant experience have not been given proper attention. Too often pedestrians are treated like trespassers in their own towns. We want streets that are decent and attractive to walk in.'

John Prescott's DETR Transport White Paper 20 July 1998

John Prescott's words show that walking is climbing back up the political agenda. But cars and lorries still dominate our lives and

the walking environment is in a sorry state. No wonder pedestrians suffer road rage! The Pedestrians Association is determined to turn the Government's commitment to walking into affordable and achievable changes on the ground.

Walking is important

1. Walking is the 'glue' binding together the transport system. It accounts for nearly a third of all journeys and 80% of journeys under a mile. Most car journeys and nearly all public transport journeys involve a walk.
2. Walking is the 'nearest activity to

perfect exercise' (*Sports Medicine*, May 1997). Walking is good for you and cuts down on unnecessary car journeys and the associated noise and air pollution.
3. Walking is also a socially sustainable means of travel. It is free and requires no special equipment. Creating safe, pleasant areas for walking is a vital part of bringing our towns and cities back to life.

But do pedestrians get the environment they deserve?

Walking remains a major mode of travel despite the appalling condition of the walking environment.

- Britain's pavements are a disgrace. Government figures show that one in five pavements are sub-standard, and the trend is worsening. People need clean, well-maintained pavements they can walk on without fear of tripping. They also need an end to pavement parking and pavement cycling.
- Pedestrian crossings, where they exist, are often in the wrong place. Pedestrians are diverted through subways, over footbridges or made to cross a road in several stages. Few towns or cities have coherent networks of pedestrian routes.
- Speeding vehicles intimidate pedestrians and annually cause thousands of deaths and injuries.

We need lower traffic speeds in our villages, towns and cities.

These conditions are particularly serious for people with mobility difficulties or sight problems. The walking environment needs to be designed and maintained to meet the needs of everyone, not just the young and able bodied.

What does the Pedestrians Association do?

From its earliest days, the Pedestrians Association has been scoring successes on behalf of pedestrians. In the 1920s, our campaigns persuaded the Government to introduce the driving test, the 30mph urban speed limit and pedestrian crossings. The Pedestrians Association also helped write the very first Highway Code.

Since those early successes we have moved on to cover all aspects of pedestrian welfare.
- We work to make walking safer, more convenient and easier, making it possible for people to leave the car at home when travelling short distances.
- We protect and promote the rights and safety of people travelling on foot and provide information and advice to the public, other organisations and the Government.
- We work with the Government, local authorities and other bodies to promote the benefits of walking as an environmentally friendly, sustainable and healthy form of transport.

© The Pedestrians Association

More cycling

A safer journey to school

Regular cycling protects against heart disease, stroke and other illnesses, and raises self-confidence and well-being.

Most children own bicycles and many would like to use them for the school journey, but very few do. Traffic danger is the main reason, with cyclists among the most vulnerable road users. But where schools have the benefit of a network of cycle routes and slower speeds, the whole picture changes, and cycling can become a popular choice for travel to school. Cycling gives children more freedom and has great benefits for health: regular cycling can add years to life.

Reducing road danger

The key to meeting safety concerns is safety measures that give a real reduction in road danger. In the Netherlands, as cycling has become safer, casualties have fallen, even though the number of people cycling has risen. Plans for changes in road layout around the school should incorporate safer cycle routes. In co-operation with the local authority and cycling organisations, schools can identify the best routes for traffic-

free and traffic-calmed cycling. This may mean clearing, surfacing and lighting muddy tracks to make them usable cycle paths, creating cycle tracks alongside roads, or marking cycle lanes on roads while enforcing slower traffic speeds. Junctions can be redesigned to give priority to cyclists. Cycle routes should be continuous.

School cycle racks

Cycle routes alone are not enough to make cycling to school a practical option. Cycle parking will be needed, preferably in a covered area overlooked by classrooms or offices, and convenient for the main entrance. Stands or racks should allow the cycle frame, and not just the front wheel, to be locked to them using a 'D-lock' or something similar. Smaller stands may be required for primary age pupils. While providing secure stands, schools need to make pupils and parents aware that if a bike is stolen the school will not be held liable. Many insurance companies will cover bicycles under a standard household contents policy, provided they are locked securely. Separate insurance

may be necessary for more expensive bikes. Postcode tagging can be carried out by local police.

Cyclist training

Young cyclists need training to prepare for riding on roads. Most local authority road safety departments offer cyclist training for children aged ten and above, and can be invited into school to run courses. Those that don't may be able to provide guidance and training to enable the school to set up its own scheme. Instructors should be experienced adult cyclists who have received training from a road safety officer. Research shows that the most effective courses are those which include on-road training. Children learn more if they take the course over several weeks rather than one or two. Problem-solving approaches, which teach 'cycling awareness', appear to make children safer cyclists than more traditional, instruction-based courses. As with pedestrian training, it is important to make it clear that courses will not automatically equip children to take to the road. These decisions have to be made in the light of local conditions and remain the responsibility of parents and children. Some road safety departments offer one-to-one training on the route between home and school. Others have run special courses for parents and children cycling together.

Safety gear and advice

Cyclists are safer if they are more visible. Schools can help by selling discounted reflective clothing and accessories. Children should be advised to carry spare batteries for lights and change them as soon as they run low. Helmets can reduce the severity of head injuries in accidents (though their effectiveness diminishes with speed). Helmets should be properly fitted, have a 'CE' mark and should meet either the European standard BS EN 1078:1997, or the American standard SNELL B95.

Maintenance checks

Cycles ridden to school should be fully roadworthy and properly maintained. Some schools offer classes in cycle repair. Road safety officers or cycling organisations can help run maintenance check-ups. It is useful if schools can keep spare sets of lights, locks, pumps and repair kits to lend to children who have lost their own, and set up a bike maintenance area.

Cycle permit schemes

Some schools operate a cycle parking permit scheme. This is a contract, drawn up between the school, the pupil and the parents, to set out the conditions for cycling to school and obtain the parents' consent. Sample permits are available (see Resource file). Permit forms set out the school's

cycling policy, while emphasising that the decision on whether the child is competent to cycle remains with the parent. Forms can also include advice on safety and insurance and provide a record of the bicycle's make and serial number. Schools need to decide what conditions they wish to attach to permits. These might, for example, include that:

- the bicycle is roadworthy and has passed a maintenance check
- the cyclist has completed an approved training course
- the bicycle will be securely locked in an approved area
- the cyclist will follow a 'good cycling code' (see Resource file).

Lockers and carriers

Schools can provide secure lockers to store cycling equipment and reduce the number of books that children have to take home. Panniers are recommended for carrying books on bikes.

Cycling events

Cycling can be promoted with special events at school such as a 'cycle challenge': children are encouraged to try out a range of cycling skills including riding slowly and around obstacles. Schools may like to take part in national events such as charity bike rides.

Routes into the community

At Kesgrave High School in Suffolk, a network of traffic-free cycle routes links nearby housing estates and enables pupils to cycle from up to five miles away without going along a main road. Around 60% of pupils come by bike, and traffic at the school

gate is kept to a minimum. Brian Hawkins, the school's deputy head, says: 'The whole of our local community is a learning resource because so many of the kids will cycle to local facilities.' The school actively encourages cycling and provides secure cycle storage and lockers.

Journey focus

At Temple Moor High School in Leeds pupils in Year 7 are offered cycle training with a special focus on the journey to school. Road safety officers ride with them pointing out potential hazards and recommending the best route.

Resource file

Right Track: Cycling awareness programme tutor's guide is available from The Royal Society for the Prevention of Accidents, Edgbaston Park, 353 Bristol Road, Birmingham B5 7ST, tel 0121 248 2000, £52.50 for a pack of 10.

Code of Good Practice: The practical aspects of cyclists' training is also available from ROSPA, price £5.

A sample school cycle parking permit is available from Sustrans with the information sheet *Cycling to School: Advice for parents and schools*. Also from Sustrans is *The Good Cycling Code*. PO Box 21, Bristol BS99 4HA, both are free of charge.

Cycle bells, reflective tabards and bands are also available from Sustrans.

Information about national cycling events is available from CTC, Cotterell House, 69 Meadrow, Godalming, Surrey, GU7 3HS, tel 01483 417217, fax 01483 426994.

The Greener Motoring Guide

A guide to more environmentally responsible motoring

Why do we need a Greener Motoring Guide?

The motor car has given us enormous opportunities in terms of mobility and freedom. However, with these opportunities come responsibilities, especially towards our environment.

The reasons are clear. The number of cars on the UK's roads is expected to rise, the number of journeys made and the distances driven each year are increasing while the number of new roads being built is decreasing.

Not surprisingly, environmental concerns voiced over air pollution grow ever louder. In urban areas, particularly, local air pollution can occasionally reach high levels and there is increasing anxiety about climate change and the need to reduce carbon dioxide (the main greenhouse gas) emissions.

So for the motor industry comes the responsibility of continuing to develop new technologies to minimise the environmental impact of the car.

For the individual motorist comes the responsibility of using the car more sensibly and intelligently.

And this is why we need a Greener Motoring Guide.

To help all of us learn to drive greener and in a more disciplined way. To make us stop and think about the way we actually drive, so that each of us, in our own small way, can make an impact. Can make a difference.

If we do this together, then we can manage the car.

On the right road

Let's get one thing straight. The motor car is not the environment-destroying monster that some people make it out to be.

Of course, car emissions do impact on air quality and climate change, but the UK motor industry has taken a leading role in tackling this problem.

Technological developments have significantly reduced emission levels, with more efficient engines, catalytic converters, cleaner fuels and recyclable materials all reaping environmental rewards.

So much so, that despite increasing numbers of cars on our roads, regulated emissions are now falling and will continue to fall for at least the next 20 years.

And the work is continuing, as technology is advancing. Indeed, it is believed that by 2010 total regulated emissions from the UK car population will have fallen to about one-quarter of their 1990 level.

It's a sure sign that car manufacturers are not only on the right road, but a long way down it.

But there is no room for complacency. Transport is an increasingly significant source of greenhouse gases and driving behaviour can make a great difference to local air quality.

In recent years, the car's environmental performance has improved dramatically. A good example is one of the UK's best-selling small cars, where it now takes 20 of them to generate the same level of regulated pollutants that one 1970s model did when it was new.

Your Greener Motoring Guide

OK, so the motor industry is making progress. But what about you, the individual motorist; how can you help? In the global scheme of things, many of you may be thinking that 'doing your bit' can't possibly make an impact. Yet if every motorist could adopt more discipline, and a little more responsibility, then collectively we can and will make a huge difference.

So why not follow the Greener Motoring Guide and play your part? No one's asking for a radical change in lifestyle, just a few small changes, here and there.

Try to drive less

Think about how you use your car. Of course, for many journeys it's an absolute necessity but often you'll get in it automatically just to pop round to a friend's or go to the shops for a paper.

For such short trips, do you really need to take it? Could you not walk, cycle or take public transport, say, once a week? You'll not only save on fuel, it might even do you some good!

Reductions in our mileage, particularly the number of short journeys made, when coupled with projected gains in new car fuel efficiency, could deliver substantial reductions in car emissions and improvements in air quality.

So be sure your journey is necessary. Why not set yourself a target to cut your annual mileage and number of short journeys? Our guide on page 34 will help you.

Service your vehicle regularly

In order to cut down emissions, your car needs to be kept in tune and serviced at regular intervals.

It is estimated that a minority of vehicles that are badly maintained or simply worn out cause the majority of all vehicle pollution.

So don't be tempted to skimp on servicing – it will probably cost you more in the long run anyway!

Older cars

Although a poorly maintained car of any age will pollute, many of the worst polluters on our roads are the oldest cars. Research has shown that if all cars more than 10 years old were taken off the road and replaced by new cars, traffic pollution could fall by up to 25 per cent immediately and up to 50 per cent by 2002.* Essentially, this is because new petrol cars are being fitted with catalytic converters which reduce polluting emissions by up to 90 per cent.

If you do drive an older car, help the environment by making sure it is tuned regularly. Should you have the opportunity to replace your car, why not choose a newer, more fuel efficient model fitted with a modern engine and catalytic converter? The Government will in the future make road tax less expensive for smaller, 'cleaner' cars.

*Source: TETRA Ltd, University of Thessalonika (1996), *Foremove Model Forecasts for the UK*.

Fuel consumption

Fuel is one of earth's most precious assets. However, when it is burnt it generates greenhouse gases which are widely believed to contribute to climate change. Keep an eye on your fuel consumption to ensure your car is running as efficiently as possible. Any increase is not only wastage but might indicate a mechanical problem.

Here are 5 steps to find your car's fuel consumption*
1. Brim the fuel tank (but do not overfill).
2. Zero the trip meter or note the mileage.
3. Drive for, say, 100 miles (make a note of the actual miles driven).
4. Brim the fuel tank again and note

the amount of fuel it takes (litres or gallons).
5. Divide the number of miles driven (say, 100) by the amount of fuel used (litres or gallons) to find your car's fuel consumption.

*This is best done on a long run with the engine at normal operating temperature.

Buy cleaner fuels

Find out about the availability of low sulphur diesel (City diesel) or cleaner petrol (low sulphur/aromatics) in your local area. The Government has changed the duty on fuels to make low sulphur diesel less expensive than ordinary diesel. So try and use cleaner fuels to reduce the amount of harmful emissions coming from your exhaust.

'Cleaner petrol and diesel products already on the market can reduce traffic exhaust emissions by up to 5 and 15 per cent for nitrogen oxides and fine particulate matter respectively.'

Source: NSCA (1998) *Cleaner Air: The Role for Cleaner Fuels*.

Slow down

Kill your speed. Not only to save lives but to save fuel. For example, driving at 70 mph can use up to 30 per cent more fuel than driving at 50 mph.

Source: DETR (1998) *New Car Fuel Consumption Figures*.

Drive smoothly

By thinking ahead you can often avoid sudden braking and sharp acceleration. This will not only reduce fuel consumption and

emissions, but help cut down on car and tyre wear. To perfect these skills, consider taking an Advanced Driving course.

'It has been estimated that à smoother driving style can bring fuel savings of 10 per cent in urban areas and 6 per cent outside urban areas.' Source: ANFIA Statement on CO_2, 2 October 1997.

Switch off

Switch off your engine whenever it is safe to do so, especially when you're stuck in traffic for long periods. Prolonged and unnecessary idling is zero miles per gallon! Also, if you have air conditioning, use it sensibly to reduce fuel consumption.

Drive off immediately

Don't warm your engine up by allowing it to idle from cold. Drive off straight away and use as high a gear as reasonable to minimise initial cold start emissions.

Check your tyre pressure

Ensure your tyres are inflated to the correct pressures, as specified in your car's handbook. For accurate readings, only check when your tyres are cold.

'Driving with tyre pressures 0.3–0.4 bar (4–6 p.s.i.) below that recommended can increase fuel consumption by 2–3 per cent.'

Source: ANFIA Statement on CO_2, 2 October 1997.

Cut down wind resistance

By removing your roof rack when not using it and keeping your windows closed, you'll cut down wind resistance and decrease fuel consumption.

'A fully loaded roof rack will increase motorway fuel consumption by 30 per cent and even a simple ski rack causes increases of 7–8 per cent.'

Source: ANFIA Statement on
CO_2, 2 October 1997.

Use your gears more efficiently

Driving in the highest gear practicable is a more efficient way of driving. For example, it is estimated that a speed of 37 mph in third gear uses 25 per cent more fuel than in fifth gear.

Source: ANFIA Statement on
CO_2, 2 October 1997.

Travel light

Remove unnecessary items from your boot to reduce weight, improve fuel consumption and reduce emissions. Unless you really need them, avoid adding heavy accessories, and wider tyres that add rolling resistance.

Plan your journey before you set off

A little planning can save you a great deal of hassle. Work out the best route to travel, always try and take familiar roads and be prepared to journey off-peak. If you have to commute, think about a Park and Ride scheme or using public transport.

'It is estimated that 20 per cent of driving time on unfamiliar roads is spent getting lost, and as a consequence, motorists waste 350,000 tonnes of fuel per year.'

Source: *Telematics Technology*,
Automobile Association, 1997.

Share trips

Can you share travel, like commuting or the school run? It will cut down on both your fuel and parking costs. Also, if you have two cars, try and use the smaller one for short trips wherever possible.

Green Transport Plans

An increasing number of employers are introducing Green Transport Plans to help reduce the number of commuter journeys that employees make by car. These include car-sharing schemes, installing cycling facilities, subsidising bus/train passes and encouraging employees to work from home via information technology. Ask your employer if such a scheme is available for you. For further information or a free briefing about Green Transport Plans, send a stamped addressed envelope marked 'GTP' to Transport 2000, Walkden House, 10 Melton Street, London, NW1 2EJ or see their publication *Changing Journeys to Work*, price £30.

Company cars

Company car drivers should try to adopt all the greener driving practices. If you drive a company car, ask your employer about the purchasing of more fuel efficient vehicles, using cleaner fuels and better planning of routes.

Learn to drive greener – your target

Target – To reduce the number of short car journeys you currently make per week by at least one, and to achieve at least a 1 per cent reduction in mileage each year.

a. How many short journeys do you currently make per week? (journeys less than 2 miles)

b. How many miles did you drive last year?

Commuting
Weekday/Weekend leisure use
Holiday mileage
Total =

For a 1% saving:
Total/100 = Annual mileage saving target

So where can you make this saving?

Think carefully. Can you share a car to work at least one day a week, travel on public transport once a week, car share on the school run? Can you walk, cycle or use public transport on short journeys? Why not ask your supermarket if they offer a home delivery service?

Set yourself a target and stick to it. If we all do our bit, we can make a difference.

For further Information

Suggested contacts:
- The Society of Motor Manufacturers and Traders Ltd, Forbes House, Halkin Street, London, SW1X 7DS
- The Automobile Association, Norfolk House, Priestly Road, Basingstoke, Hampshire, RG24 9NY Royal Automobile Club, 14 Cockspur Street, London, SW1Y 5BL
- The Department of the Environment, Transport and the Regions, Romney House, 43 Marsham Street, London, SW1P 3PY
- Institute of Advanced Motorists, IAM House, 359-365 Chiswick High Road, London, W4 4HS
- British School of Motoring Group Plc, 81-87 Hartfield Road, Wimbledon, London, SW19 3TJ National Rail Enquiries: Telephone (0345) 484950
- The offices of your vehicle manufacturer
- The Environmental Health Department of your local authority Transport 2000, Walkden House, 10 Melton Street, London NW1 2EJ.

The car that will save the world

It sounds like a fridge, and produces no more pollution than a kettle. Andrew English drives the world's first five-seat, zero-emission, fuel cell car

Sorry, but the water-powered car does not exist, perpetual motion is impossible, Superman can't fly and I'm even having my doubts about Father Christmas. So when I'm presented with a car that will save the planet, I remove my rose-tinted spectacles and take a long, hard, cynical look. Cars, and the individual mobility and freedom they represent, will always have their price in lives, pollution and the destruction of the world's resources; if we accept the principle, we can work to reduce the price.

But this week the price fell sharply with the launch of Daimler Chrysler's NECAR 4: the first five-seat, fuel cell-powered car. As American Environmental Protection Agency (EPA) administrator Carol Browner rather cutely put it: 'This vehicle leaves just a trail of water vapour as it drives by, not hydro-carbons or carbon monoxide. Those who inherit the next century will look back on our efforts with gratitude and in good health.'

NECAR 4 will probably be the last fuel cell concept car Daimler Chrysler produces before a production version goes on sale in 2004. It is a 90mph, 60-65mpg, five-seat Mercedes A-Class, with twin Ballard Power Systems fuel cells mounted under the floor, providing electricity to a conventional electric motor under the bonnet. The fuel cells use cooled liquid hydrogen, stored in a sort of giant Thermos flask in the back of the vehicle, and give a range of around 280 miles between refills.

As to whether this is what you'll be able to buy in 2004, assuming the company keeps to its self-imposed deadlines, that remains to be seen. For although fuel cells have been known about for 160 years, their use in cars has been only recent and a lot of unanswered ifs and buts remain.

It wasn't just right-on cycling administrator Browner making fantastical claims at the launch in the Ronald Reagan International Trade Center in Washington. Daimler Chrysler co-chairman Robert Eaton, a man who has made squillions out of the merger of the two companies, spouted on about Chrysler's contribution to fuel cells, when in fact they are almost all Daimler's work. 'It's the next step in a long journey we've been on for some time,' he waffled from his prepared speech; American journalists lapped it up, but by then Eaton had reached the far corners of his performance envelope and had to hand over to a man who really knows his stuff, co-chairman Juergen Schrempp.

'What will the production fuel cell car be like on the road?' he was asked. 'It will be like any Mercedes – safe and fast,' he snapped, his square spectacles glinting menacingly. 'We will apply our full technological power to develop environmental vehicles,' he warned, 'and we are trying to remain "fuel neutral" and open a dialogue with the oil companies.'

> **'This vehicle leaves just a trail of water vapour as it drives by, not hydrocarbons or carbon monoxide. Those who inherit the next century will look back with gratitude and in good health'**

And there lies the biggest 'but' about the whole enterprise; fuel cells run on hydrogen, but where do you get the hydrogen from? Although carrying hydrogen (derived from natural gas) in the car is the simplest and cleanest solution, it is also highly volatile. While the dashing head of the Daimler Chrysler fuel cell project, Dr Ferdinand Panik, outlined a potential $1.4 billion programme to install hydrogen fuelling facilities at 30 per cent of the gas stations in the three US states which are proposing zero-emissions regulations (California, New York and Massachusetts), it was hard not to think about the last time the Germans demonstrated advanced hydrogen technology in America: May 6, 1937, when the airship *Hindenburg* exploded in New Jersey, killing 33 passengers and crew.

Even in the ultra-modern NECAR, hydrogen is vented from the tanks at a rate of one per cent of the volume per day if the highly pressurised liquid fuel becomes too warm. For a production car, that vented fuel would be stored in metal hydrides in a sealed tank, but even so, there is a limited amount of time you can leave a liquid hydrogen-fuelled car without the whole thing going 'pop!'

Which is where methanol and petrol come in. It is possible to 'reform' methanol or even petrol into hydrogen on board the car, but the reforming process raises pollutant levels. A static model of a production methanol-fuelled fuel cell NECAR was shown at the launch, with a reformer under the floor along with the fuel cell. While using methanol reformed from natural gas, the whole process from source to power at the car's wheels cuts a petrol engine's carbon dioxide (CO_2) 'greenhouse gas' emissions by 30 per cent and city polluting oxides of nitrogen (NOx) and poisonous carbon monoxide (CO) by up to 80 per cent. Modifying the aforementioned filling stations to supply methanol would cost only $400 million.

Before the merger with Daimler, Chrysler mooted the idea of reforming petrol on board in 1997 but while Daimler Chrysler was keeping its options open, Dr Panik clearly didn't think much of the idea; he didn't even include source-to-wheels efficiency figures in the blurb, even though changing those filling stations to provide the designer-brewed petrol would cost a mere $200 million.

And if that weren't enough to think about, there is also the threat of highly efficient diesel engines, such as the one in the 94mpg Volkswagen Lupo we tested last year (3/10/98), which are not only cheaper but on sale this year – and give the cleanest hydrogen-powered fuel cell car a close run for its money in source-to-wheels efficiency figures.

There are also design challenges still to meet with the fuel cell: its weight (around 660lb too heavy), its cost and the risks of freezing in cold weather and overheating in hot weather.

With all that in mind I climbed into the NECAR alongside a Mercedes boffin who had been installed to prevent me crashing the thing. Starting up is a slightly fussy process. You turn the key round two positions and wait a couple of seconds for the systems to activate, indicated by a series of lamps on the dashboard. With another key turn the systems check begins, which ends a couple of seconds later with all the lights going off. You know the systems are operating, because the fuel cell's air compressor pump starts to rumble under the floor.

Engage drive on the gearbox selector (there is no gearbox for the electric motor), press the throttle and with a noise like a stricken cow from the compressor, we're off.

Daimler claims that this, the sixth series fuel cell vehicle it has built, has improved acceleration, top speed, range and refinement over its predecessor, NECAR 3. From a

standing start the acceleration is brisk if not tyre rippling. The electric motor whirrs and the air compressor groans louder as you floor the throttle. NECAR feels heavy when you try to turn into a corner and the suspension is stiff over bumpy roads, but it feels stable and, even at 50mph, it accelerates eagerly.

Occasionally, hidden sensors detect water building up in the fuel cell and the compressor roars loudly as it purges the system, which is pretty startling; future compressors may have to run harder and longer to help provide a reservoir of hydrogen for quick acceleration.

There's a lot still to do and a lot still to be learned about fuel cell cars; they really aren't up to saving the world just yet and the conventional piston engine still has some environmental developments in store; the war has definitely not been won. Nevertheless, Daimler Chrysler is determined to retain its technological lead and put a fuel cell car into production in five years. And it is that pledge, together with a working NECAR 4, that made this such an impressive demonstration.

But why did they chose to launch such an environmentally sound vehicle in a land where petrol costs 70 pence a gallon, cars around two-thirds what we pay in the UK and nearly half the 15 million new vehicles sold each year are gargantuan-engined off-roaders? Juergen Schrempp was bullish about

the benefits of free enterprise in developing environmental vehicles, as opposed to government regulation, but even he admitted that 'incentives may be needed' if the American public are to buy any NECARs at all. Faced with a lot of questions about this, he and Eaton whizzed off to do more friendly network television interviews and it was left to the still, calm voice of Chrysler's senior vice president for engineering technology, Bernard Robertson (coincidentally a Brit) to tell it like it is.

'We have called for environmental fuel tax increases in the past, but as it was a political non-starter over here, we stopped talking about it,' he said. 'There is simply no market for environmentally friendly vehicles in the States, but then who knows how long gas is going to remain at 80 cents a gallon? We simply can't go on building big iron-block V8s indefinitely; you lot would rightly flay us alive for that. If we can just get the NECAR's price down and the package right, then we'll have done our job. After that, it's up to the politicians.'

I wasn't the only journalist who, at that point, went searching for a politician to answer some questions about the US government's policy on fuel tax. You wouldn't have thought it too difficult to find one just yards from the White House, but, strangely, they had all disappeared . . .

National Car-Free Day

Information from the Environmental Transport Association (ETA)

What is National Car-Free Day?

National Car-Free Day (CFD), co-ordinated by the Environmental Transport Association, is about encouraging people to voluntarily leave their cars at home for a day and experience the benefits of other forms of transport!

National Car-Free Day has arisen from the rapidly growing CFD movement. Born in Bath in ETA Green Transport Week (GTW) 1995, it spread to over a dozen cities in GTW 96, and went national for the first time in 1997 with nearly 100 participating towns and cities. *Review of 1997 CFD and GTW*

CFD organisers from across Britain planned for CFD 99 which was on Tuesday 8 June 1999.

National Car-Free Day will be the focal point for ETA Green Transport Week (also co-ordinated by the ETA). 2000 dates will be announced.

CFD and GTW will focus the public's attention on the damage caused to their health and local environment by increased dependence on the private car. Awareness is raised in local communities throughout Britain. The benefits of cycling, walking and using public transport are exposed in a spirit of community involvement and fun.

The CFD message is fourfold:

Environment, road safety, health, community

There are many opportunities for communities to unite and get involved in issues which concern everybody.

CFD is not, and should not appear to be, a local authority dictat. Community involvement and ownership is crucial – though of course local council participation, and funding, will be invaluable.

Organising your own car-free day

Identify your aims for the day, and how they fit into the wider transport strategy for the area.

Recognise that CFD is largely an awareness-raising event – do not expect sudden traffic and pollution drops of 50%, and you will not be disappointed.

Involve as many sections of the community as possible

Schools: schoolchildren are not only the country's future motorists, but also have considerable influence over their parents!

Local businesses: employers have a potentially significant influence over local transport use, and the journeys made by their employees to work.

Public transport operators: local bus and train operators can be approached to provide special offers on the day (and throughout GTW).

Health authorities: the health benefits of more cycling and walking coupled with less pollution are potentially vast. Local clinics, GP surgeries and hospitals should all support CFD.

Environmental groups: a likely source of assistance in organising the event(s).

Other local community groups: the civic society; chamber of commerce; residents' associations; police; parish councils; cycling clubs and campaigns; women's groups... etc. Involve as many as you can – don't forget, many of them will be willing to help you run things!

The local media: keep them informed at all stages. Ideally involve them in the CFD planning committee, inviting them to all meetings. Media co-operation is crucial, given that CFD is chiefly about raising awareness.

Structuring the organisation

Form a steering group to oversee the strategy, with representatives from the council and groups mentioned above.

Form sub-groups to address the detail of different topics: publicity, schools involvement, public transport, cycling and walking, and special events or competitions. (Sub-groups then report back to the main group. This format helps keep the main group focused on strategy without becoming bogged down in detail – it also helps keep meetings short!)

Take care to elect the right chair for your CFD organisation: someone who is well known and respected and has energy and enthusiasm. Ideally s/he will also be a good spokesperson for the event when the media come banging on doors for interviews.

Involve the media right from the start: it is crucial to maintain a good working relationship. Invite local media to be present at the main strategy group and the publicity sub-group meetings.

Ideas for events

Some events and activities which have proved successful in past years are listed below. Not all of them will be appropriate for a particular community or area. Try not to do too much – it is better to focus on a few well-organised events than to spread activities and resources too thinly.

Local business

Commuter journeys account for one in four of all car journeys made, and the car is the most common means of travelling to work. Write to prominent local public and private employers early on, encouraging them to take part in CFD. Highlight the potential long-term benefits to business of reduced car use, e.g. the potential savings on company cars and company car parks, a fitter, less stressed workforce, etc. etc. Arrange seminars or workshops showing local employers how to operate a green transport policy in their companies. Suggest in your letters to company chairmen the following ways for their businesses to get involved:

- Introduce flexible working hours and dress, making it easier for employees to walk or cycle.

- Provide changing facilities if possible, and badges to show support for CFD.
- Think about allowing employees to work from home, thus obviating the need for any commuting at all.
- The CFD challenge – which department is the greenest? Allocate red and green stars to individuals according to their mode of transport to work that day. Prizes and booby prizes.
- Encourage company PR departments to seek media attention for their efforts. Good media coverage will be good for business!

Schools involvement

- In 1970, 80% of schoolchildren aged 9-11 made their own way to school, mostly by bike or on foot. That figure has now plunged to 9%.
- The main reason parents give for ferrying their kids to school by car is road danger. So they drive and add to the traffic . . . This vicious circle must be reversed.
- Approach schools early
- Schools have a lot to do and you will need to keep their involvement simple.
- Circulate letters to schools in your area inviting them to take part, outlining a proposed activity, such as:
- Walk to School Week (15-19 June) – phone the Pedestrians Association on 0171 490 0750 for details.
- Safe Routes to Schools: children will often come up with the best ideas for road safety improve-

ments to the roads they have to use every day.
- Greenest School Competition – survey of travel to local schools (both on a normal day and on CFD). Prize for the greenest school.
- Greenest Class Competition – as above but contained within one school. Prize for the greenest class.
- 'Green Miles' – the number of miles travelled to school by car is subtracted from those travelled by 'bus, bike and walking. Any positive scores get a voucher redeemable against fuel for school minibus/coach company equivalent to the number of Green Miles obtained.
- Road Chain – the class or school makes a map of where everyone lives, and a walk to school is organised with the furthest away starting first and picking up people on the way. The result is lines of friends all weaving their way to the playground. Try to engage the co-operation of the local community policeman.
- Organise a special breakfast for pupils who arrive on foot, cycle, pony, go-kart, roller blades . . .
- National Car-Free Day and ETA Green Transport Week poster competitions – could be sponsored by a local bike shop – win a mountain bike.
- Banner-making workshop for publicising GTW and CFD.
- Presentations to schools on green transport, Local Agenda 21, cycling, road safety and road danger.
- Packs to schools including badges,

colouring sheets, posters and leaflets.
- Involve parents and governing bodies – early!
- Encourage schools to seek media attention for their efforts, or offer to do this for them. Kids love to get into the local papers – and editors love to have them there!

In the town centre

Many stunts have been employed to involve the wider public, most of which use the town centre as a focus. Different events will be best run by different types of groups:

Voluntary groups, e.g. local branch of Friends of the Earth, city cycling campaign, can run:
- City centre CFD/GTW exhibitions
- Exhibition of vintage transport or new transport technology.
- Dr Bike cycle safety checks.
- Gentle 45-minute lunchtime cycle rides using cycle routes.
- Workshops and seminars covering topics such as local transport policy, green transport for individuals and business, car-sharing clubs.

Local authority
- Road safety roadshow.
- Promotion of cycle paths and alternative pedestrian routes.
- Promotion of park and ride initiatives, with provision of maps and information.

Other
- Health fitness tests by local health authority.

- Street entertainment – uni-cycling display etc.
- Secondhand bike stall – sell or buy – local bike shop.
- Bike postcoding by local police.

Public transport
- Negotiate special ticket offers with local public transport operators – e.g. two tickets for the price of one, special reductions, flat rates all day, day rover tickets etc. Ensure good advance publicity.
- Local council could use the day to launch a park-and-ride scheme.
- Be wary of street or car park closures – the CFD message is more effective if participation is voluntary. Alienating the public or the emergency services is the last thing we want to achieve!

Cycling and walking
- Provide and publicise extra bicycle parking to encourage cycling into the town or city centre.
- Organise a short evening family cycle ride to highlight new routes (or the need for new routes). End with a picnic in a local park, or at a family-friendly pub with garden.
- Organise an urban family walk, as above.
- Use CFD/GTW to publish and distribute information on recommended safe cycle and pedestrian routes.

Car sharing
- Encourage essential car-users to initiate a car-share scheme.
- Provide posters to stick in car windows, publicising the fact that they are car sharing.

Launching positive measures
- Use the day to launch new and positive measures such as new cycle routes, park and ride schemes etc.
- Make sure the local media are coming.
- Invite a local celebrity to cut any ribbons.

Publicity
Good publicity – and plenty of it – in the weeks prior to CFD is the key to a successful event. CFD is nothing if people do not realise it is happening.

The importance of involving the media from the start has already been emphasised. Make sure you prepare a good press release, explaining what, why, where and when as briefly and clearly as possible. Include a few soundbite quotes, as from your chairperson. Don't forget to include at least two phone numbers for the press to contact you. Other means of publicising CFD include:
- Leaflets: to schools, libraries and other public buildings using the council's own internal mail distribution system. Also to shops, bus and rail stations, cars in car parks . . .
- Posters: as above, plus – high street windows, on public transport, at car park pay and display meters, public buildings . . .
- Street banners: relatively cheap, can be hugely effective.
- Temporary road signs: ditto.
- Internet: use the local council's web site.
- Advertising: negotiate special rates in local newspapers.
- Local press/radio/TV interviews.
- Articles in the local paper, featuring the CFD logo where possible.
- Letters to schools, employers and doctors' surgeries.
- Articles for local group news-letters, e.g. Chamber of Commerce.

An official launch should be considered – probably towards the end of May, or early June. Arrange a press photo shoot, with suitably photogenic opportunity. Have slogans and soundbites ready!

All promotional material should briefly explain the objectives of CFD – copy from this information – and should ideally use local statistics that will highlight local problems and local concern.

Last, but not least: inform the ETA! Preferably email a copy of your press release to pascale@compuserve. com or fax it to 01932 829015.

The ETA will publicise your event along with all other GTW and CFD events to both regional and national press and of course on their web site.

Use of National Car-Free Day logo
All publicity should feature the National Car-Free Day logo. This will help link your event with the hundreds of others expected to be running on the same day across Britain.

The logo can be customised to your local town, city or county, e.g. Bath Car-Free Day. The logo is available in colour. To discuss logo options and place an order, please phone the ETA on: 01932 828882

Monitoring
Monitoring should not be over-looked: you should be able to report on your achievements, both to the media and your backers.

A well-organised monitoring procedure is an essential part of a good campaign. According to resources available, monitor the following:
- awareness of CFD – do people know it's happening?
- media coverage – total air time and column inches
- traffic counts on major routes
- numbers of tickets sold at car parks
- car occupancy rates (for evidence of car-sharing)
- cyclist counts
- air quality

Do not forget to monitor things like traffic and pollution levels on a normal day, ideally with similar weather conditions (perhaps the same day of the previous or following week) so that reasonable comparisons can be drawn.

When to start planning
Now!
The earlier you get the ball rolling, the more you will achieve – and the less last-minute panic there will be. A suggested month-by-month guide to planning your CFD events is given below:
- Nov/Dec – identify aims and targets, people to be involved, elect chairperson.
- Jan/Feb – decide budget, research and plan activities, start designing publicity.
- March/April – approach local schools and employers, finalise publicity.

- May – official launch with local press, start distributing publicity.
- June – publicity, monitoring.

Finance and budgeting

CFD can be run – and has been run in past years – on shoestring budgets. Obviously more can be achieved and things can run more smoothly with more funds. But all is not lost if you have got less than you were counting on – a good campaign in the first year for instance may well secure a larger budget for future years.

After the event

A proper thank you event – perhaps a civic reception – will be well received by everyone involved in your CFD, and will help solidify relationships between organisers. This will be especially useful when it comes round to planning for the following year – and starting all over again!

Further information

This information has been assembled using ideas that have worked in past years in various CFD events around Britain.

It has attempted to distil a lot of work by a lot of people into an easy-to-follow guide to getting your event off the ground. Its aim is to help future CFD organisers to get on with the task in hand, without wasting precious time and resources re-inventing wheels. We hope you find it useful.

If you would like further information, or copies of any background literature used to compile the information (e.g. leaflets and posters, example letters to businesses and schools etc., all of which can safely be cribbed – nothing is copyright) please contact the ETA on the phone number given below.

The Environmental Transport Association is Britain's only provider of breakdown and recovery cover which campaigns for environmentally sound transport. Its fast and reliable breakdown service at competitive prices allows motorists who are concerned about the environment to buy their peace of mind from an alternative to the motoring organisations, who form part of Britain's immensely powerful road lobby. The ETA also operates Britain's first recovery service for cyclists.

For details of the ETA's services: ETA, 10 Church Street, Weybridge, KT13 8RS. Telephone: 0193 282 8882. Fax: 0193 282 9015. E-mail: info@eta.co.uk Web site: http://www.eta.co.uk

© ETA Services Ltd

Choosing and using a cleaner car

Motor vehicles are a major source of air pollution. Rapid growth in vehicle use means that efforts to reduce emissions from individual vehicles are in danger of being overtaken by the increase in volume of traffic. However you can choose a car and use it in a way that reduces pollution. This information examines the relative merits of vehicles currently available – secondhand petrol cars, new petrol cars with a three-way catalytic converter, diesel cars and diesels with an oxidation catalyst.

Using a cleaner car

The smaller and lighter a car is, the less fuel it uses, therefore CO_2 emissions are lower. Fuel consumption and emission levels are also affected by speed, the most efficient speed being 40–55 mph. Emissions from vehicles are highest when engines are cold. In hot weather a petrol car may have to be driven for 6 miles in an urban area before the engine is fully warmed and operating efficiently – in cold conditions it will be even longer. In a petrol car the catalyst must reach operational temperature before it is effective. In the UK 40% of journeys are under 3 miles. For journeys of less than a mile emissions from a petrol car with catalyst may be fourteen times higher than those from a diesel car. Emissions of CO and HC increase with congestion for petrol, while for diesel there is little difference. Emissions for NOx in congested traffic are lowest for petrol cars with catalysts and similar for diesel and petrol without catalysts.

Choosing a car

The car you choose will depend on the following factors:
1. The importance you attach to the various pollutants – are you more concerned about local health effects and particulate pollution or global warming?
2. How much more are you prepared to pay for an environmentally friendlier car – consider fuel economy and ease of maintenance.
3. Are you prepared to sacrifice comfort and personal status by choosing a smaller car?

Driving patterns and maintenance have to be taken into account when assessing the amount of pollution a vehicle will emit, so it is important to keep the following points in mind:
1. Maintain the vehicle regularly, checking tuning, emission control and tyre pressure. Dispose of old engine oil properly.
2. Reduce unnecessary journeys. Short trips use a lot of fuel, especially if the engine is cold – walk, cycle or use public transport where appropriate.
3. Drive gently – racing starts and sudden stops increase fuel consumption.
4. Drive more slowly – a self-imposed speed limit of 60 mph will reduce emissions and save fuel.
5. If stuck in traffic for more than a minute, switch off the engine.

© NSCA October 1999

ADDITIONAL RESOURCES

You might like to contact the following organisations for further information. Due to the increasing cost of postage, many organisations cannot respond to enquiries unless they receive a stamped, addressed envelope.

Bicycle Association
Starley House
Eaton Road
Coventry, CV1 2FH
Tel: 02476 553838
Fax: 02476 228366
The Bicycle Association is the national body representing the manufacturers and importers of bicycles, components and accessories.

British Roads Federation (BRF)
Pillar House
194-202 Old Kent Road
London, SE1 5TG
Tel: 0171 703 9769
Fax: 0171 701 0029
E-mail: brf@brf.com
Web site: www.brf.co.uk
Campaigns in the UK for a safe and efficient road system as part of a coherent transport strategy. It is not anti-public transport, nor anti-rail. Publishes reports, books and leaflets.

Council for the Protection of Rural England (CPRE)
Warwick House
25 Buckingham Palace Road
London, SW1W 0PP
Tel: 0171 976 6433
Fax: 0171 976 6373
E-mail: cpre@gn.apc.uk
Web site: www.greenchannel/com/cpre
Conservation of the English countryside. Keeps readers abreast of current issues and promotes positive solutions. Ask for their publications catalogue.

Environmental Transport Association (ETA)
10 Church Street
Weybridge, KT13 8RS
Tel: 01932 828882
Fax: 01932 829015
E-mail: eta@eta.co.uk
Web site: www.eta.co.uk
The ETA an alternative to the AA and RAC. They campaign for a more sustainable and integrated transport system.

Friends of the Earth
26-28 Underwood Street
London, N1 7JQ
Tel: 0171 490 1555
Fax: 0171 490 0881
E-mail: info@foe.co.uk
Web site: www.foe.co.uk
As an independent environmental group, Friends of the Earth publishes a comprehensive range of leaflets, books and in-depth briefings and reports.

National Society for Clean Air and Environmental Protection (NSCA)
136 North Street
Brighton, BN1 1RG
Tel: 01273 326 313
Fax: 01273 735802
E-mail: info@nsca.org.uk
Web site: www3.mistral.co.uk/cleanair
NSCA's objectives are to promote clean air through the reduction of air, water and land pollution, noise and other contaminants, while having due regard for other aspects of the environment. The society examines environmental policy issues from an air quality perspective and aims to place them in a broader social and economic context. Publishes comprehensive and contemporary information for the public and educational material.

Pedestrians Association
31-33 Bondway
London, SW8 1SJ
Tel: 0171 820 1010
Fax: 0171 820 8208
E-mail: info@pedestrians.org.uk
Web site: www.pedestrians.org.uk
The Pedestrians Association works to make walking safer, more convenient and easier, making it possible for more people to leave the car at home when travelling short distances. Protects and promotes the rights and safety of people travelling on foot and provides information and advice to the public, other organisations and

the Government. Produces newsletters, student packs and reports. Contact them to purchase a schools pack for the Walk to School Campaign Week which will be held 22-26 May 2000 and 25-29 September 2000.

Society of Motor Manufacturers and Traders Limited (SMMT)
Forbes House
Halkin Street
London, SW1X 7DS
Tel: 0171 235 7000
Fax: 0171 235 7112
Web site: www.smmt.co.uk
Publishes factsheets, newsletters, student packs, reports and briefings.

Sustrans
35 King Street
Bristol, BS1 4DZ
Tel: 0117 929 0888
Fax: 0117 929 4173
E-mail: info@sustrans.org.uk
Web site: www.sustrans.org.uk
Sustrans works through practical projects – such as the National Cycle Network and Safe Routes to Schools – to design and build routes for cyclists and walkers. Its National Cycle Network aims to provide an 8,000-mile network of cycle routes throughout the UK. Sustrans produces a wide range of cycling-related information.

The Automobile Association (AA)
Norfolk House
Priestly Road
Basingstoke, RG24 9NY
Tel: 01256 492192
Web site: www.theaa.co.uk
The objectives of the AA are: to promote safety on the roads; to represent the interests of road-users; to provide services and benefits to members; and to assist in harmonising the needs of road-users with the protection and enhancement of the environment. Please note that the AA does not have the resources to deal with individual student enquiries.

INDEX

The Internet has been likened to shopping in a supermarket without aisles. The press of a button on a Web browser can bring up thousands of sites but working your way through them to find what you want can involve long and frustrating on-line searches.

And unfortunately many sites contain inaccurate, misleading or heavily biased information. Our researchers have therefore undertaken an extensive analysis to bring you a selection of quality Web site addresses.

* * * * *

National Society for Clean Air and Environmental Protection (NSCA)
www3.mistral.co.uk/cleanair
Click on the NSCA Information button which will take you to the following links: FAQs, Leaflets, Factsheets and Other sources. All of these are worth checking out. Their site contains numerous useful articles on vehicle pollution.

The Automobile Association (AA)
www.theaa.co.uk
Entering your key words in the Search field, such as pollution or congestion, leads to a variety of useful articles. Combining a key word search with the scroll down menu to News & Views in the Shortcuts field also produces some useful information.

Environmental Transport Association (ETA)
www.eta.co.uk
The Environmental Transport Association organises Green Transport Week and Car-Free Day each year. Their web site has numerous articles/factsheets relating to these two campaigns. A very informative site.

Sustrans
www.sustrans.org.uk
Sustrans – it stands for sustainable transport – is a charity working on practical projects to encourage people to walk and cycle more, so as to reduce motor traffic and its adverse effects. Their web site is a must for anyone interested in cycling.

Society of Motor Manufacturers and Traders Limited (SMMT)
www.smmt.co.uk
SMMT offers a wide range of information and advice. The UK Motor Industry Facts 99 document (Adobe PDF format) and The Green Motoring Guide can be downloaded.

British Roads Federation (BRF)
www.brf.co.uk
The BRF is a business organisation representing users and providers of the road network in the United Kingdom. Click on Press Releases and News for their views on transport issues.

ACKNOWLEDGEMENTS

The publisher is grateful for permission to reproduce the following material.

While every care has been taken to trace and acknowledge copyright, the publisher tenders its apology for any accidental infringement or where copyright has proved untraceable. The publisher would be pleased to come to a suitable arrangement in any such case with the rightful owner.

Chapter One: Current Trends

What's the problem with traffic?, © Friends of the Earth, *Vehicles and drivers*, © British Roads Federation, *Roads and the environment*, © British Roads Federation, *Pollutant emissions*, © British Roads Federation, *UK loves to drive but hates to pay the cost*, © The Guardian, June 1999, *How we compare*, © The Guardian, June 1999, *Transport: what are the issues for the countryside?*, © Council for the Protection of Rural England (CPRE), 1999, *Rural traffic fear survey*, © Council for the Protection of Rural England (CPRE), 1999, *England's countryside*, © Council for the Protection of Rural England (CPRE), 1999, *The tranquil areas of England*, © Council for the Protection of Rural England (CPRE) 1999, *Britain faces 10 years of traffic chaos*, © The Guardian, June 1999, *City drivers face £7,000-a-year charges*, © Telegraph Group Limited, London 1999, *Motor vehicle pollution*, © National Society of Clean Air and Environmental Protection (NSCA), *Safe Routes to Schools*, © Sustrans, *Ten facts about children and roads*, © Crown copyright material is reproduced with the permission of the Controller of Her Majesty's Stationery Office, *Parking ban demanded to halt school run chaos*, © Telegraph Group Limited, London 1999, *Journeys to school by main means of travel*, © Automobile Association (AA), *The evolution of Reclaim the Streets*, © Reclaim the Streets (RTS), *Fair deal?*, © Automobile Association (AA), *Council 'waste millions on public transport'*, © Telegraph Group Limited, London 1999, *End of the road for park and ride?*, © Andrew Baxter, *Alternatives to driving*, © MORI (Market & Opinion Research International Ltd.).

Chapter Two: Seeking Solutions

All aboard for better bus and train services, © The Audit Commission, *Better buses*, © Crown copyright material is reproduced with the permission of the Controller of Her Majesty's Stationery Office, *Bike for your life*, © Bicycle Association, *Health benefits*, © National Cycling Forum, April 1999, *More walking*, © Crown copyright material is reproduced with the permission of the Controller of Her Majesty's Stationery Office, *Walking to School*, © Automobile Association (AA), *When walking do you suffer road rage?*, © Pedestrians' Association, *More cycling*, © Crown copyright material is reproduced with the permission of the Controller of Her Majesty's Stationery Office, *The Greener Motoring Guide*, © Society of Motor Manufacturers and Traders Ltd. 1998, *The car that will save the world*, © Telegraph Group Limited, London 1999, *National Car-Free Day*, © Environmental Transport Association (ETA), *Choosing and using a cleaner car*, © National Society of Clean Air and Environmental Protection (NSCA).

Photographs and illustrations:

Pages 1, 7, 10, 14, 31, 32, 36: Pumpkin House, pages 2, 4, 11, 12, 21, 23, 33, 34, 38: Simon Kneebone.

Craig Donnellan,
Cambridge
January, 2000